DECLUTTERING YOUR HOME

Tips, Techniques & Trade Secrets

DECLUTTERING YOUR HOME

Tips, Techniques & Trade Secrets

Geralin Thomas

FIREFLY BOOKS

A FIREFLY BOOK

Published by Firefly Books Ltd. 2015

Copyright © 2015 Quarto Inc.

First printing

Publisher Cataloging-in-Publication Data (U.S.)

Thomas, Geralin
Decluttering your home : 200 tips, techniques and trade secrets / Geralin Thomas.
[176] pages : color photographs ; cm.
Includes index.
Summary: "How to free your home, computer and calendar of clutter and maintain an organized environment and lifestyle" – Provided by publisher.
ISBN-13: 978-1-77085-585-4 (pbk.)
1. Storage in the home. 2. Orderliness. 3. House cleaning.   I. Title.
648.8 dc23   TX309.T466 2015

Library and Archives Canada Cataloguing in Publication

Thomas, Geralin, author
Decluttering your home : 200 tips, techniques and trade secrets / Geralin Thomas.
Includes index.
ISBN 978-1-77085-585-4 (paperback)
1. Orderliness. 2. Storage in the home. 3. House cleaning. 4. Organization. I. Title
TX309.T46 2015 648'.8 C2015-903828-6

Published in the United States by
Firefly Books (U.S.) Inc.
P.O. Box 1338, Ellicott Station
Buffalo, New York 14205

Published in Canada by Firefly Books Ltd.
50 Staples Avenue, Unit 1
Richmond Hill, Ontario L4B 0A7

Color separation in Hong Kong by
Cypress Colours (HK) Limited

Printed in China by
1010 Printing International Limited

Conceived, designed and produced by
Quarto Publishing plc
The Old Brewery,
6 Blundell Street, London N7 9BH

Senior editor: Claire Waite Brown
Senior art editor: Emma Clayton
Designer: Karin Skånberg
Design assistant: Martina Calvio
Picture researcher: Sarah Bell
Illustrators: Josh @ KJAArtists.com
Kuo Kang Chen
Art director: Caroline Guest
Proofreader: Sarah Hoggett
Editorial assistant: Georgia Cherry
Indexer: Diana LeCore
Creative director: Moira Clinch
Publisher: Paul Carslake

Contents

74. Master bedroom

82. Closets

110. Craft/hobby space

114. Packing for vacation

> 66 In character, in manner, in
> style, in all things, the supreme
> excellence is simplicity. 99
>
> *Henry Wadsworth Longfellow*

Welcome to my world

Ask me to simplify your complicated, chaotic, disorganized stuff—from calendars to collections, to wardrobes and wandering thoughts—and you'll make me happy. Since starting my North Carolina-based home-organizing business in 2002, I've helped clients all over the world create lifestyles that reflect who they are, despite their organizing challenges. While some need help transforming their chaotic home into a tranquil haven, others want to take their organizing accessories from drab to fab, find things in a minute or less, live simpler lives or experience pride and pleasure every time they walk through the door of their home. Being organized helps people live healthier, happier, more productive lives.

I SHOULD KNOW

I've been like this my whole life! When I was a young girl, my Barbie doll wasn't a jetsetter; she enjoyed "staycation" days during which she organized her life from the comfort of her own camper and dream home. I took the time to rearrange her evening gowns, handbags and small but envious shoe collection. Fast forward to the 1990s when, as a new mother of two boys born 14 months apart, I had to be organized to survive. Friends and acquaintances told me that my systems and methods of organizing inspired and helped them; they wanted me to teach them how to organize their garages, files, new businesses and events. Over the years, I've shared my secrets and sources via my blog, books and TV appearances.

TIME FOR A TRUE CONFESSION

Just like my clients, I occasionally procrastinate when I need downtime. My favorite ways are through social media such as Instagram, Pinterest, Facebook, Twitter, LinkedIn and Google+. And often I find that I learn while I'm relaxing.

Feel free to join me! To learn more about me, my business or where we can connect socially, visit my website, www. MetropolitanOrganizing.com.

About this book

n recent times, reality TV shows highlighting hoarding tendencies have raised awareness about keeping too much stuff. As a result, decluttering and organizing are now trendy topics. You're with the in-crowd if you've started buying experiences in lieu of material gifts. The travel and hospitality industries are experiencing a boom in business from those who have grown weary of buying more "stuff" to "stuff" in their already "stuffed" homes, and who have cleaned up their calendars to make room for fun. Homeowners are still spending money, but instead of buying

knickknacks and whatnots, they're choosing theater tickets, spa treatments and amusement-park passes.

People are eager to learn how to live with less, practice minimalism and enjoy a less stressful lifestyle. How to declutter and de-stress is the new hot topic that can be brought up in any conversation. It's as if decluttering is a sport, and everyone, regardless of age, income or gender, is welcome to play along and beat clutter.

This book is a culmination of the best ideas I've learned about decluttering and organizing as both an on- and off-

01 CLUTTER, CLUTTER EVERYWHERE
Pages 12–25

Dealing with clutter can feel very overwhelming. This chapter provides the foundation of the book: the what, where, why, when, and how of clutter.

02 HOUSEHOLD CLUTTER
Pages 26–115

This chapter takes you through organizing the home and eliminating household clutter, room by room.

Information is presented in easy-to-access units, so you never feel overwhelmed

Great photographs are subjected to analysis

Plenty of tips and great advice

camera organizing expert. My goal in writing this book is to teach you how to transform your casa de C.H.A.O.S (Can't Have Anyone Over Syndrome) into casa de calm. I want to replace confusion with confidence. Life is better when we live in a well-ordered home that suits our lifestyle and expresses our personality. We are content when we create a hospitable habitat, one where we treasure our time spent.

With each chapter you'll find advice to help you decide what you can live with as well as what you can live without. Together, we'll create a house that looks attractive and feels inviting and comfortable, keeping only the items and activities that reflect you and what's most meaningful to you. The process of getting organized becomes much more pleasurable when it's viewed as an opportunity to let go of things, respecting who you are now, where you've been and where you want to be.

This book is filled with trade secrets, resources, tips, tools, tactics, techniques and organization revelations.

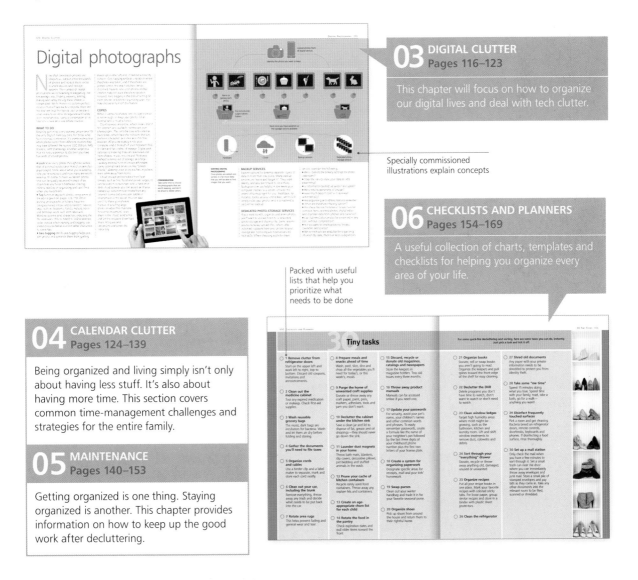

03 DIGITAL CLUTTER
Pages 116–123

This chapter will focus on how to organize our digital lives and deal with tech clutter.

Specially commissioned illustrations explain concepts

06 CHECKLISTS AND PLANNERS
Pages 154–169

A useful collection of charts, templates and checklists for helping you organize every area of your life.

Packed with useful lists that help you prioritize what needs to be done

04 CALENDAR CLUTTER
Pages 124–139

Being organized and living simply isn't only about having less stuff. It's also about having more time. This section covers common time-management challenges and strategies for the entire family.

05 MAINTENANCE
Pages 140–153

Getting organized is one thing. Staying organized is another. This chapter provides information on how to keep up the good work after decluttering.

CLUTTER, CLUTTER EVERYWHERE

01

Before decluttering can begin, it is useful to consider why you need to declutter, where the clutter has come from and how you might be affected when it comes to letting go. In this chapter you will learn how to cope with what seems to be an overwhelming task, and what to do to cure clutter.

Psychology of clutter

Clutter comes in multiple forms and flavors; it's everywhere, but have you ever stopped to wonder why we have so much stuff? Most of us, even those who live simple lives, enjoy buying and owning things: homes; cars; memorabilia; clothes; furniture; jewelry; or collections of vinyl albums, stamps or porcelain dolls. But there is a difference between stuff that we need and clutter.

▪ **Utility** Certain items allow us to accomplish a task more efficiently, and our homes are filled with utilitarian objects. For example, a snow shovel helps us remove snow from walkways, which helps us take control of our environment. We feel a little more powerful over something that we really don't have too much power over—the weather. So, owning a shovel is useful and lets us feel empowered.

▪ **Identity** Some of our stuff helps identify who we are; it's a silent signal broadcasting a message about us. T-shirts with logos immediately identify which brands we like, groups we belong to or causes we support. By owning certain items we project part of our personality and our capabilities. If the man next door owns the greatest and latest electronic devices, we might assume he's tech-savvy, and those gadgets must somehow enhance his life. I might see him as my go-to guy if I can't reset my Wi-Fi password. His identity is enriched in our eyes by owning these things, just as if we went to someone's home for the first time and noticed bookshelves filled with biographies of American presidents. We would assume the reader is a history buff or interested in American politics. The books help that person maintain their identity and preserve their past, since they have been collecting these books and reading them for many years.

▪ **Security and comfort** Some of the objects we own give us a sense of security. Like toddlers who snuggle a stuffed animal or cuddle a blanket to comfort themselves, as adults we fill our homes with comfort items—things that make us feel good. We might choose one piece of furniture over all the other options because it's plush, and when we sit, we sink into a cozy cocoon. Even the intangibles, such as a specific scent or flavor, are capable of transporting us back in time to a pleasant memory of feeling secure and comforted.

YOUR REACTIONS TO STUFF

Items that people buy or acquire—whether passively or intentionally—awaken different emotions and feelings, depending on personality type. Creative people often claim that having their tools out in plain sight is the key to keeping their energy flowing; bouquets of millinery flowers or a kaleidoscope of colorful markers might inspire them. They prefer to keep things out in the open for inspiration and because out of sight is out of mind, so when they can't see their stuff they forget it is there.

Others are most productive with a clean slate. They are the "fresh start" people that begin or end their days by clearing everything from a work surface or arranging things in order. They subscribe to the "everything has a place" system, and love checklists. They gravitate toward tried-and-true methods, as opposed to constantly craving novelty.

Regardless of your personality type, you can always find a system for organizing the stuff you use, that identifies you

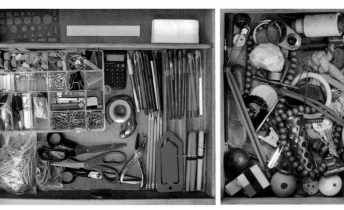

MAKING DECISIONS
Before you can organize your life and your home, you need to figure out which of your possessions you really need.

and that gives you security and comfort. But before you can do that, you need to understand the difference between these items and clutter.

WHAT IS CLUTTER?

Many people find it difficult to describe clutter. We know it when we see it, and we can almost always give specific examples, but defining it is complicated. I like to describe clutter using "uns." Items that fall into any of these "un" categories can be described as clutter, for example:

- **Unused** Obsolete floppy disks.
- **Unwanted** The tall ceramic King Neptune that Aunt Bertie painted in her ceramics class.
- **Unloved** The dozens of pens and pencils stashed in drawers; an old bridesmaid dress; freebie tote bags.
- **Undecided** Charity solicitation requests; event invitations.
- **Unfinished** An incomplete craft project; a shirt waiting for a button to be sewn on.

When you look at your stuff in light of the "uns," you start to determine what is useful and what is merely clutter.

WHERE DOES CLUTTER COME FROM?

Clutter enters our lives in many ways, shapes and forms. Typically we purchase it or acquire it.

- **It was a bargain** The fact is it's easier than ever to accumulate things. Every town seems to have either a big-box discount store or a store that sells everything for 99 cents. We buy things we don't need just because they seem like a bargain. When the store in town isn't open, we can shop online all day, every day. And we don't need cash! Using a credit card to buy online removes us from the negative "spending" feeling and instead emphasizes the positive emotion of "receiving." As an added incentive, many sites offer free shipping, making it that much harder for us to control our impulses.
- **It was useful, once** When you bought that treadmill you had every intention of using it each day, but now it sits collecting dust and has piles of clothes and books on top of it. You probably, mistakenly, think you will use it again.
- **It was given to me** We often inherit clutter from well-meaning relatives who assume we are happy to have a too-big-for-our-house dining room table or an ugly vase because "it needs to stay in the family!" We feel it would be unkind or ungrateful to refuse, so in our home it becomes something that is unwanted and unloved, but still there.

...I have stuff therefore I am!

Will I feel insecure?

...my stuff empowers me...

My stuff makes me happy...

Should I clear everything away for a fresh start?

Who am I?

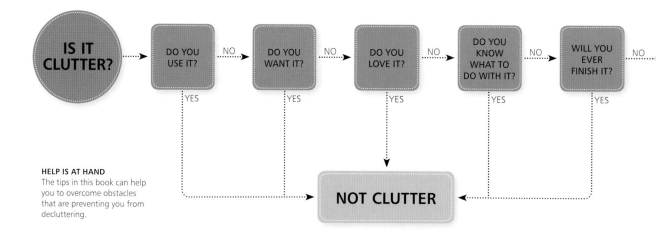

HELP IS AT HAND
The tips in this book can help you to overcome obstacles that are preventing you from decluttering.

■ **It was free** Conventions and expos are excellent sources for clutter acquisition. Who can resist a free visor, plastic water bottle or pen? Throw a few business cards and colorful brochures in, and it's a recipe for countertop clutter.

Cosmetic companies supply us with clutter and lots of it, especially around Mother's Day and Christmas. Some of our favorite brands offer a GWP (gift with purchase), which includes an adorable little bag filled with samples of things most women can't or won't wear. These items soon become bathroom-drawer clutter.

Just because something is free, it doesn't mean we will use it. Nevertheless, when you are offered something for free, it can be difficult to say "no."

■ **It was sent to me, so it must be useful** Clutter does not have to be physical. Today's modern lifestyle requires us to manage unprinted photos, rapid-fire emails, print-on-demand documents, multiple phone numbers with multiple voicemail accounts, and a ceaseless ticker of texts reminding us that a flash sale is happening three blocks from us and our car repair, hair-salon and dental appointments await us.

We gather email messages, software programs we use once then never again, and multiple files that we are afraid to "trash." Applying the rules of "uns" to our digital lives will show just how much clutter there is on our desktops. And we aren't entirely to blame for this type of clutter conundrum, since data miners and advertisers do their homework, gathering intelligence on our preferences and sending us messages that suggest they want to help us save money or feel better about ourselves. What they really want us to do is spend MORE money, on their products.

I CAN'T GIVE IT AWAY BECAUSE

We have already discovered that items gather in the home from a variety of sources. But, if we don't use them, want them or love them, why do we keep them?

■ **I feel guilty** Anyone who has wasted money on something they haven't used as much as they thought they would—for example, that juicer that's too much trouble to clean—feels terrible about having spent all that money. That guilt prevents you from donating the item, and so it becomes clutter.

■ **I feel obligated** Are you hanging on to a gift from a dear friend to avoid hurting that person's feelings? Perhaps an item has been passed down to you from a family member, and you are holding on to it to pass to your children, who probably don't want it either.

■ **I will use it someday** If you have a barely used treadmill collecting dust and you think you will, eventually, use it again, you're hopeful. If you're saving "trophy sizes" (clothes you used to slip into comfortably two sizes ago), you're optimistic that they'll fit again. But the truth is, if you did fit into that size again, you'd probably want to buy new stuff.

■ **I might need it someday** Believing that we may one day need to provide documentation to prove a point—store receipts; insurance documents; tax records—leads us to feel we need to keep all sorts of paperwork, "just in case."

WHEN YOU KNOW IT'S CLUTTER

These sources of clutter can creep up on us. At first we think we will use the things we are holding on to, perhaps they will save us money, or be useful in the future. However, if you come to realize that you really don't need them, don't use them, don't love them or don't know what to do with them, you need to consider decluttering, and the benefits it will have on your whole life (see The Benefits of Decluttering, page 18).

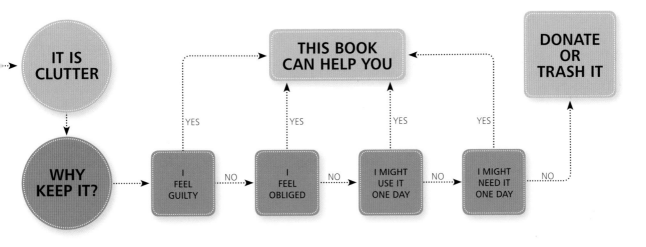

Effects of clutter

A disorganized home negatively affects all aspects of a person's wellbeing, from their physical and emotional health to their finances.

PHYSICAL EFFECTS OF CLUTTER

Disorganized, overstuffed spaces increase the likelihood that inhabitants will suffer from allergies to excess dust or mold. In addition to allergens, cluttered homes are a haven for germs and bacteria, and the risk of fire and injuries increases as more stuff is accumulated and piled on staircases or next to fireplaces, kitchen stoves or other sources of heat. Plus, not being able to find things when they're needed can put hurdles in someone's routine—heading to the gym but, "I can't find my running shoes!" or heading to a job interview but, "Where are my keys?"

EMOTIONAL EFFECTS OF CLUTTER

Disorganization increases stress and anxiety, as a home feels out of control and cramped instead of peaceful and relaxing. Homeowners become overwhelmed and aren't sure where or how to begin. Those with significant amounts of clutter tend to either procrastinate because the effort required to make a change feels overwhelming, or they avoid it altogether. A disorganized home may even discourage someone from inviting friends, family and neighbors in, or worse, not allowing repairmen in because they are too embarrassed.

FINANCIAL EFFECTS OF CLUTTER

Clutter becomes costly. Paperwork is a common clutter culprit; overlooked invoices, unopened applications and rebates or ignored bank statements may languish on an entryway table or kitchen counter for months. These delays and missed deadlines incur late fees and overdraft charges. Even a disorganized pantry and refrigerator can end up costing its owner hundreds of dollars a year because uneaten leftovers, expired canned goods and wilted produce contribute to exceeding one's annual grocery budget.

Having more stuff than space can really hurt household budgets when individuals rent storage units; the expenses add up. The average cost of a medium-sized storage unit is $100 per month. Therefore, it's important to make sure the belongings taking up space in a home are worth keeping. Do the math and figure out how much it would cost to buy new items instead of storing them over a long period of time. Storage units are wonderful as temporary solutions—for example, if you're having wood floors refinished and need to get everything out of the house for two weeks, or a college student needs to store dorm furniture over the summer break—but having one for many years is not a worthwhile investment.

The benefits of decluttering

D o you feel calm, comfortable and relaxed in your home? Would you like to have more time and more money? Clutter affects your bank account, your happiness and your health, but when you make a habit of letting go of the unwanted and unnecessary, and keeping your life in order, your wallet will be fuller, you'll have more time to enjoy life and you'll love your home.

CLUTTER'S EFFECTS ON YOUR EMOTIONS
Let's start with how clutter in the home, on the computer or in your schedule affects you personally, and the negative emotions you experience as a result of not being organized.

■ **Irritation** Are you often irritated or grumpy because you don't have systems in place that allow you to relax and enjoy an afternoon reading on the couch?
■ **Embarrassment** Do you have "doorbell dread" and want to hide whenever someone turns up unexpectedly for a visit? Do you cringe inwardly each time you ask a friend to resend a document because you can't find anything on your computer? Or perhaps you are hugely embarrassed because you are always late for appointments, or worse yet, you miss them altogether?
■ **Guilt** Do you forget the dates of games, recitals and potluck suppers? Were you mortified to have missed your son's recital, or your good friend's baby shower?
■ **Frustration** Are you constantly frustrated at being unable to perform specific tasks because the items you need have gone missing?
■ **Exhaustion** Does it feel like you have more to manage every day? More laundry, more activities, more paperwork to complete and phone calls to return, with no break in sight?
No matter how the clutter has accumulated, decluttering is a process everyone can tackle

VISUALIZE THE WELL-ORGANIZED HOME Imagine being able to easily find what you need in your closet (below), or being able to set out dinner plates without first having to clear a space on the kitchen table (top right).

that will address the negative ways it may make us feel. The advice I give in this book will mean you no longer have to deal with these unwanted feelings and frustrations. An organized home and lifestyle will instead leave you feeling content, calm and in control.

TAKE CONTROL
The main benefit of decluttering and organizing is that it allows you to take back control of your

home and your everyday life. Let's start with your wardrobe. Every day millions of people look in their stuffed closets and think, "I've got nothing to wear." Organized people have plenty to wear. Wouldn't it be incredibly liberating, emotionally and financially, to take control of clutter and reach a point where everything in your closet fits well, feels and looks good, and projects a true image of who you are?

Decluttering means you free yourself of the unnecessary, which in turn means you can always find what you need. As well as saving on feelings of frustration, you will also be saving yourself time when you can find things effortlessly, without searching in the trunk under the bed or the closet in the basement.

You can also take control of your time by pruning events from your calendar (see Saying "No," pages 128–129). Just as decluttering shelves, countertops and cabinets frees up space in the home, clearing the clutter from your schedule gives you valuable free time to spend how you choose, putting you in control of your time.

FINANCIAL BENEFITS OF A CLUTTER-FREE EXISTENCE

The crux to decluttering lies in clearing out what you don't need, want or love. Your stuff is then weaned to a manageable amount, and organized in a way that means you can find things easily. The first financial benefit you will notice when this is done is that you don't waste money on duplicates. In a disorganized environment, when you need something but can't find it (you know you have one, but where is it?), you buy another one, and another one,

and another one. One day, you decide to get organized and discover you have six pairs of scissors and nine pairs of reading glasses.

Getting organized with your paperwork will benefit your finances by ensuring you don't incur late fees on overdue items, misplaced bills or forgotten deadlines. Plus, if you plan ahead you are more likely to get good deals, on train or airline tickets, for example.

When your calendar is organized you will find you save money—and time—on regular shopping trips. Shopping without a detailed list, forgetting items or purchasing the wrong thing squanders time and money. By organizing your time through weekly planning (see page 131) you know exactly what needs to be bought, when and by whom, so there are no duplicates, or emergency trips back out when you remember at the last minute that you promised to make your dad a birthday cake.

Keeping the clutter in check can also help you to manage the home finances more efficiently. The old you, in finding the shoes you bought online are too small, might have put the box in a pile of other "projects" that you intend to get around to on the dining table, for example. The pile gets added to by all members of the household, and the shoes get lost and forgotten about. The longer you leave them there, that's another month you are out of pocket—or they may never get returned at all. The organized you, on the other hand, won't have a pile of "projects" on the dining room table, so the shoes can't get lost, plus you will have checked your calendar, or put a note in your action file (see page 92), and decided on a time to take the shoes to the delivery depot.

The many benefits

Take a moment to imagine all the other benefits you will experience as an organized person.

Pride Invite guests into your home without anxiety, and enjoy hosting.

Relaxation Live this simple equation: Mess-less = stress-less. The more you say no to recreational shopping and acquiring, the more time you'll have to do what you want to do.

Health Deciding to live a less complicated life often results in having more money, enjoying more free time and also practicing better self-care.

Model behavior You'll become a role model for those around you, including little ones you think aren't paying attention. Model organized behaviors and let your kids learn by example.

Safety Move freely through your home with easier access to hallways, staircases and doorways.

Personality types

Everyone has a unique style in the way he or she collects and manages specific types of belongings or clutter. While some people struggle with an overabundance of clothing (they enjoy shopping for the latest styles and always seem to find good deals), others collect items related to their hobbies, tech toys, craft supplies and books. Then there are homeowners who can't part with sentimental items, inherited belongings, family photos or anything their children created.

The objects of someone's affection have more to do with individual personalities, interests and hobbies than most people think. For better or worse, the items we surround ourselves with reflect our personal preferences and priorities. But keeping stuff comes at a cost.

The clutter personality quiz

I created this clutter personality quiz to help you identify the kind of clutter you accumulate and why. It will help you learn which areas of your home are likely to need the most attention and how to approach your unique decluttering and organizing challenges.

1 What do you like to shop for most?
A The grab-and-go shopper: You stop into stores only for what you need. You're a shopping efficiency expert and can be in and out of the grocery store in 15 minutes or less.
B The extreme reader: Your e-reader is almost as full as your bookshelves. You can't resist stopping in bookstores, grabbing a coffee and picking up something new to read.
C The tech guru: You're an early adopter and would definitely camp out on the sidewalk waiting for a new iPhone release.
D The shopping shunner: You don't like crowds, detest malls and prefer to do all shopping online.
E The bargainista: No one can scout out a sale like you. Bargain basements and discount stores are your favorite spots. Your prized possession is your coupon collection.

2 What kind of clutter can you simply not part with?
A The "I'll use it someday" items.
B Old books, new books, books you'll never read (love me, love my books).
C Cables, cords, chargers and all electronic accessories (hey, they're still good).
D Sentimental items and family photos (even the bad ones).
E Coupon clippings, junk mail and paper pileups (these can be dealt with later).

THE "OUT OF SIGHT, OUT OF MIND" CLUTTERER

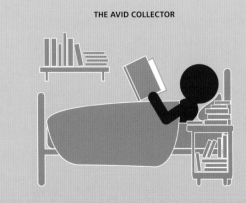

THE AVID COLLECTOR

3 What are the most cluttered areas of your home?
A Corners, cabinets and closets.
B Shelves, bookcases and nightstands.
C Desk drawers, kitchen drawers, nightstand drawers.
D Walls, guest rooms and storage spaces.
E Pantry, office and garage.

4 What stops you from decluttering?
A "I've got better things to do."
B "I have plans to use it."
C "I think I can sell it."
D "I can't throw away my family's memories."
E "I don't have time."

5 Which best describes your home?
A Your home is mostly organized, but clutter lurks behind every closet door.
B You're a pile maker. Horizontal surfaces are a magnet for clutter.
C You make every drawer an "everything drawer."
D You make room on your walls for every photo and art project.
E You can't remember when you last had enough room in your garage for your car.

REVIEW YOUR ANSWERS
The chances are that you circled the same letter more than once. Here's how your personality type tends to accumulate clutter:

Mostly "A"s: The "out of sight, out of mind" clutterer
Your houseguests would never guess what clutter lurks behind your closet doors. Decluttering isn't a priority for you. Instead, you store items in your closets and cabinets.
■ **Your solution** Declutter for a few minutes every day. If you don't have time for big organizing projects, try to stay on top of things with tiny tasks (see page 146).

Mostly "B"s: The avid collector
You love to read. Newspapers and magazines pile up on your coffee table. Books are stacked high next to your bed. You love to learn but are constantly dealing with "stuff" on every horizontal surface in your home.
■ **Your solution** Choose a particular number of books to keep for rereading. Get an e-reader and buy new books that way. Recycle the newspaper every evening and throw away magazines that are more than three months old. Gift your books to other readers. Share with a friend or donate old books to your local public library.

Mostly "C"s: The techie clutterer
You're constantly asked for computer help from friends and family. Your drawers are filled with old electronics, gadgets, cords and batteries.
■ **Your solution** Set a date and review your collection. Donate, consign or throw away obsolete items and those that you no longer use. Try to use the "one thing in, one thing out" strategy. If you buy a new tech toy, give away or toss an older item.

Mostly "D"s: The saver
You serve as your family's historian. You keep all the photo albums, art projects and baby clothes. You value tradition and cherish sentimental items.
■ **Your solution** You can treasure your family's memories without keeping every single item. Keep only your favorite things. Take a photo of the others and create a digital memory photo book, which you can share with others.

Mostly "E"s: The savvy shopper
You know how to find a bargain. Your pantry is stocked with bulk-bought canned food and dry goods. You almost never pay full price and enjoy finding a good deal.
Your solution A bargain is only valuable if you planned on purchasing the item anyway. Pare down your coupon collection and think twice before buying new stuff.

THE TECHIE CLUTTERER

THE SAVER

THE SAVVY SHOPPER

The first steps

Given the choice, would you rather own less and spend less time organizing it, or own more and spend too much time looking for it? If you favor the former, having fewer things and more free time, the secret lies in organization.

It helps to understand that decluttering is not the same as organizing. Decluttering is step one of organizing. It means reducing the amount of clutter and making sure not to add more. After decluttering, you can organize what you have and you will be able to find it quickly and easily. Organizing without first decluttering is a temporary solution, a repetitive exercise of rearranging the clutter.

Decluttering is about letting go of possessions. It encourages us to evaluate what is most meaningful to us. It also frees up cash that otherwise might be spent on containers and storage units.

QUESTIONS TO ASK WHEN DECLUTTERING

How do I start decluttering? You have already taken the first step by purchasing this book, which provides plenty of advice on strategies and methods of decluttering that are relevant to the various rooms of the home, to the comings and goings of our everyday life and to the clutter that accumulates on our computers. But the very first step lies in you figuring out which items in the home are clutter. To do this, at any stage of your decluttering journey, ask yourself these questions:

- Do I love this?
- Do I use this?
- Do I need to keep it for legal or financial reasons?
- If it's not working, is it worth fixing?
- Is it worth the space it occupies?

- Could I find it on the Internet?
- Could I easily replace it or borrow it?

Remember, decluttering is not complicated. No special skills or talents are needed to declutter. Decluttering simplifies life, enabling us to live a less stressful existence. Taking time to figure out which things to let go of and what stuff is important enough to keep has an additional benefit—it raises awareness about what's being brought into the home. As you declutter, remain strong in your commitment to stop clutter from entering your home. First, declutter! Second, stop clutter in its tracks if it tries to slip back in.

ORGANIZING STARTS WITH DECLUTTERING

Decluttering is not the same thing as organizing, but it is the first step in the process of getting organized. When it comes to tangible clutter, the perfect places to start minimizing and decluttering are storage units, attics, garages and basements. First of all, there's an added advantage that some of the stuff is already boxed and ready to donate to people who will actually benefit from owning these items. Why not start there? Plus, if the boxes have been stored and unopened for years, it proves the point that we don't need what's inside.

In the case of storage units, you will benefit instantly from a financial saving. However, if the idea of sorting through the garage stops you in your tracks, because it is a huge job that overwhelms you, you might prefer to start on another room in the house, on a job that is more manageable and less daunting (see Prioritizing, pages 126–127). Once you've made a start, you may well get really into the flow and start enjoying the results so much that you want to keep going.

Quick fixes for common clutter culprits

Here are some ideas for dealing with some of the most common clutter sources I have seen again and again. Refer to page 156 for a list of items you can declutter without having to think about it.

1 Old magazines, newspapers and cookbooks

Chances are you've got one or two magazines on your coffee table that are more than three months old, and no longer relevant. Similarly with newspapers: If you don't have time to read it today, you're not going to read it tomorrow. Go ahead and toss it in the recycle bin; the news is served fresh 24/7 online! Cookbooks with complicated recipes and hard-to-find ingredients aren't worth the shelf space they are taking up, so let them go. Your favorite recipes are the ones you make over and over. If you're craving variety, look no further than your keyboard, where thousands of recipes await you online.

2 Travel-size toiletries

If you can't resist taking home small bottles of shampoo after staying in a hotel, put them to good use. Put one night's supply of soap, shampoo and conditioner in a ziplock bag. Store it in your luggage for your next trip. Then place the rest of your tiny toiletry collection in a basket for overnight houseguests to use. If you still have leftovers, donate them to your local homeless shelter.

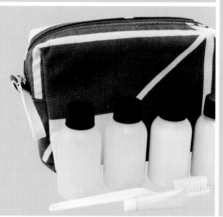

3 Clothing, shoes and accessories

There's an adage that says you wear 20 percent of your closet 80 percent of the time. Space in closets is too valuable to waste. Get rid of items that are uncomfortable, unflattering or unwanted. If your clothing is in good shape, consider consigning or donating items to a local charity.

4 Old makeup and expired medication

Take a peek in your medicine cabinet and beneath your bathroom sink. Throw out expired medications and keep only the items needed for a basic home first-aid kit. Then take a hard look at your cosmetic collection. Toss old lipstick, foundation and mascara.

5 Wire hangers

The dry-cleaner may send your suits home on cheap wire hangers, but that doesn't mean you should use them. Transfer your freshly laundered clothing onto wood hangers in your closet, and return old hangers to the dry cleaner.

6 Cabinet clutter

Food storage containers, old takeout containers, plastic stadium cups and assorted coffee mugs take up valuable space in your kitchen cabinets. Donate or throw away mismatched items. Recycle. Purchase uniform food storage containers—square, stacking, interlocking—and one set of mugs.

7 Bargains, sale items and BOGOs (Buy One, Get One)

An item on the sale rack triggers a "buy now" response. However, just because you're getting a good deal doesn't mean buying it is the best decision. It's better to pay full price for something you love than to pay half price for something you'll never use. Even if something is free, think twice before accepting it.

8 Promotional trinkets

If you go to a conference, you'll be inundated with branded pens, T-shirts and stress balls. As you visit booths, either politely decline their offer or leave them behind in a conference room. They are rarely used and quickly become excess clutter.

LABELS CAN HELP

To help you through the process, regardless of what room you are working in, make yourself some labels. The basic labels you'll need to get started are: Keep, Sell, Trash, Recycle, Donate, Relocate, Return and Shred.

Some specific rooms often have a few different labels, which are detailed on the relevant pages. Make sure you have a box or bag for each category, then sort items into your labeled containers and follow through with moving them to their proper place in the home or to the donation center. Return borrowed items and store purchases.

DISCIPLINE, NOT DEPRIVATION

While decluttering calls for self-discipline, it is not about suffering or going without creature comforts. Challenge yourself to keep only what's necessary to live a comfortable, happy, healthy life. Once you start ruminating on how much energy, time, money and attention you've spent in the past on clothes, cleaning products, herbal teas or anything else you've accumulated, you might feel any number of emotions (see Psychology of Clutter, page 14). Let go of those negative feelings and focus on specific boundaries. For example, challenge yourself to pare down everything, large and small, such as the number of teas in your kitchen cabinet, your T-shirt collection or some of the hand tools in your garage.

You'll most likely keep your favorites and discover life goes on without the others. Self-imposed boundaries help us practice self-control. Experiment by limiting the number of hangers in your closet, reusable grocery bags in the trunk of your car or anything else you have multiples of; get creative and exercise your decluttering and decision-making muscles.

THINGS TO REMEMBER

- **Decluttering is different than tidying**
Contrary to popular belief, a messy desk, home or car doesn't necessarily mean the person who uses it is disorganized. There are plenty of intelligent, creative people who aren't bothered by being surrounded by piles of their stuff. What is important is that what surrounds them is useful and wanted, and that, although it may not be obvious to an outsider, they know where everything is.
- **Decluttering is different than cleaning** While it is much easier to clean a clutter-free home, there are plenty of people who, despite thousands of emails (electronic clutter) and boxes of unfiled paperwork (physical clutter) and more than 200 magnets stuck to their fridge (visual clutter), still manage to scrub their showers, toilets and sinks, do the dishes daily and vacuum the floors.

Basic principles of organization

Once the decluttering has been done, you can turn your attention to organizing the useful, loved and necessary stuff you have retained so that you always know where to find it. There are lots of tips relating to organization throughout the book, but, if you want to become an organizing evangelist, there are some basic principles to consider.

LIKE WITH LIKE

The first organization principle is to put like with like. For example, in the bathroom keep hair paraphernalia, like combs and clips together. If you're organizing drinking glasses, it makes sense to have them all in the same cupboard. Within the glasses cabinet you can group them further, still like with like—for example, wine glasses together, next to the beer glasses next to the cocktail glasses.

PERMANENT RESTING PLACE

The second principle of organizing is that everything must have a "permanent

4 Simple rules to get you started

These tips will help you get started, but are also worth remembering in your everyday situations, to make keeping clutter at bay an easier, less overwhelming task.

1 Remember
You aren't expected to keep things that aren't meaningful to you, including monogrammed items, gifts from loved ones (you love the giver, not the gift), wedding gifts and family heirlooms that aren't to your taste. If you're a partygoer not a party-thrower, there's no need to have dozens of serving platters "just in case" or because they were given to you by dearly loved sorority sisters.

2 Keep horizontal surfaces (including the floor) tidy
Whether it's the dining-room or coffee table, kitchen or bathroom countertops, staircase or kitchen islands, always put things back where they belong when you're done using them, instead of letting them pile up.

3 Keep a donation box handy
When you have the urge, the box, or basket, is there and anything can be thrown in.

4 Numbers game
Deciding how many of each item to keep is a useful strategy to consider when you begin decluttering. If your number is three, for example, you would keep no more than three swimsuits, three tubes of lipstick, three pairs of sunglasses, three bottles of perfume, three nightgowns and three pairs of winter gloves.

address" within a home. Things can't just sit around or be shuffled from surface to surface or container to container. They need to belong somewhere, whether neatly tidied away on a shelf, hanging on a hook, tucked away in a drawer or visible on a tabletop or desk. The key is that everyone in the household knows that this is an item's home, and returns the item to its home after use.

COLOR CODING
Colors can be used to indicate categories. For example, you might store seasonal items in a box with a colored lid that corresponds, in your mind, to that season. Alternatively, you could use a color to indicate a particular family member: for example, the purple basket might be for your daughter's cuddly toys, or for anything that has migrated around the home but needs to be returned to her bedroom. You could even buy backpacks and bath towels in that color to save on muddles.

HOUSEHOLD CLUTTER

02

Organizing your home, room by room, is not going to happen just because you've purchased eye-catching containers or diminished junk in the junk drawer. An overall decluttering process needs to take place first. In this chapter you'll learn how to break down projects, how to zone rooms, how to figure out what you need and what you don't, and how to store the keepers.

Entryway

Whether through a formal foyer or a mudroom side door, the entrance to the home is much more than a passageway. It's a place where friends and family come and go, and where acquaintances catch their first glimpse into our world.

After a long day, entering home sweet home and leaving the outside world behind you should feel wonderful. For this reason, the point of entry into the home is a great place to start creating order. An ordered space within the home at the point where we transition physically and emotionally from exterior to interior, from public to private, brings comfort, joy and wellbeing.

INS AND OUTS

The entryway is typically one of the most challenging areas for homeowners to keep tidy and orderly, regardless of size, shape or style. It may be long and narrow, short and wide, contemporary, traditional or modern. Whether it is well thought out or cramped and chaotic, it becomes a repository for backpacks, boots, pet accessories, keys, hats and coats. With a little planning, however, it can be an organized, practical space in which we experience great beginnings and happy endings every day.

As you broach the task of decluttering the entryway to your home, ask yourself these key questions:

- What needs to be here? And I mean *needs* to be here—items that are used at least once a week, every week.
- What are my/my partner's/my children's habits when passing through the space?
- Do I want my stuff visible or behind closed doors?

Do I need this here, now? Look around any mudroom or entryway and what do you see? Heavy wool jackets and fur boots? Trench coats and umbrellas? Windbreakers, golf shoes and a sun hat? The contents of an entryway change seasonally, so with every season comes a fresh opportunity to reconsider what's being saved, stored and used there.

CLEAR THROUGH
Your front entryway might not be the one your family uses every day, so you may not need hooks for coats or cubbies for shoes. You still want to keep clutter at bay to ensure a clear and safe thoroughfare, so use practical solutions for everything you keep there.

Therefore, several times a year, stop and ask if there's room for improvement. Perform clutter audits and inspect everything in the space, evaluating its usefulness and purpose. Have children outgrown footwear or outerwear? Are garments still being used? Is there a closet or trunk away from the entryway where out-of-season items can be stored until needed again?

Work with your habits The ways we use the entryway reveal a lot about our organizing habits and style. While some walk in and immediately kick off their shoes, others prefer to have a seat while they remove them. There's no need to fight what comes naturally! Instead, find solutions that work with your individual habits and lifestyle. For example, if you like to sit down to remove your shoes, by all means include a chair near the door. If the mudroom

door is being used as the to-and-fro door for the family dog walker, it makes sense to keep cleanup towels handy for muddy paws.

Inside or out? Perhaps you prefer to hide the trappings of your comings and goings behind a closet door, or in a blanket box or chest—in an apartment that is short on space, for example, or in a grand entranceway in which coats and bags would look out of place. Or does everything need to be visible for easy access, while still looking neat and uncluttered? There are solutions for everyone out there, from repurposed containers to custom-built cupboards: just take the time to ensure that you will use what you choose.

SOLUTIONS TO SUIT YOU
A comfy bench (opposite) provides cushioned seating for slipping in and out of footwear. A combination of open and covered baskets adds storage space above and below. A colorful, well-organized life starts the minute kids enter the back door (above left). Jackets, shoes, backpacks and water bottles—everything has a home that is clear to see. Wall brackets support reasonably priced closet components and allow for add-on accessories as budgets permit (above). Ventilated shelving and drawers encourage airflow.

13 Ways to an efficient exit

There are many ways to control the common causes of entryway clutter. Putting things in their place as you come into the home will not only keep the entryway welcoming and accessible, but will also make leaving the house a much quicker and more pleasant experience.

1 Shoes
If shoes are typically kicked off, a complicated shoe cubby system or boxes with lids probably isn't your solution. Instead, work with habits and try one large basket or box per person. In small spaces, a rack system is easy to use.

2 Drip-dry boots
A peg system is great for storing boots upside down, so that air can circulate around them to help them dry, and any mud is kept in check.

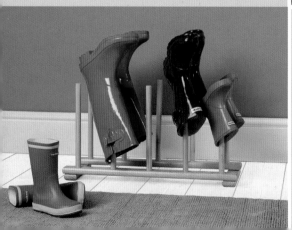

3 Close enough
Children come and go several times a day. In a perfect world, shoes would be returned to baskets and cubbies. However, if the goal is to have everyone remove their shoes before entering the house, adopting a "good enough" attitude goes a long way when things aren't perfectly placed.

4 Coats
No coat closet? No problem. Wall-mounted hooks hung at different heights make double use of vertical space in narrow hallways with limited floor space.

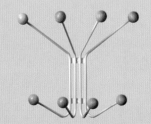

5 Book bags and backpacks

School-kid clutter starts in Pre-K and continues for a dozen years. Rather than littering the floor, install two hooks per child, one hung low for backpacks and another higher, but still reachable, for coats.

6 Keys to please

Get into the habit of hanging keys on a key hanger or placing them in a bowl or on a tray immediately after entering any outside door. Knowing where your keys are almost guarantees hassle-free departures: it's more difficult to get out the door on time if your keys are hiding in the sofa cushion.

7 Totes

Tote bags with handles can be held together with binder or carabiner clips, making them grab-n-go easy.

8 Pet paraphernalia

Leashes, collars, harnesses and plastic pick-up bags are just a few possessions of pampered pooches. Install a "hound hook" for leashes. Durable galvanized steel buckets are paw-some solutions for pet toiletries and toys.

9 Life's little essentials

Spare change, lip balm, sunglasses and headphones are easily seen and ready to go when stashed in a transparent overdoor pocket organizer.

10 Gentle reminders

Need to remind a family member to return a borrowed book or take insect repellent with them as they head out the door? A shower caddy hung over a doorknob easily contains stuff for family-style stash and dash.

11 Umbrellas

Use a deep, upright container that won't wilt when wet by house umbrellas. There are plenty of ready-made options available, in a style to suit your entryway decor. You could even repurpose a butter churn barrel or a florist's flower bucket.

12 Summer and winter accessories

Sunglasses, swim goggles and winter wear, such as gloves and scarves, rotate regularly as seasons change. A unique piece of furniture that belies its basic function can house what is required; you could even allocate one drawer per person or per type of accessory.

13 Bicycles

Bikes are commonly stored inside hallways of apartments. A great way to save space and keep the entryway neat is to mount your bike on a wall. An attractive bike mount won't look out of place.

Living room

The living room (here meaning also the den or family room) is typically a room that serves multiple purposes and hosts a variety of activities. The living room reveals a different story about those who use the space.

THE ROLE OF THE ROOM
Common living-room activities include reading, watching TV and listening to music. In addition, a living room may occasionally host overnight guests on the couch. It may also function as a kids' playroom (with toys); a music room (with amplifiers, instruments and music stands); or/ and a games room (with controllers, decks of cards, board games and puzzle pieces). It may be a room where arts, crafts, homework or exercises are done. In short, the living room is where we "live" life, and, as such, it needs to multitask—just like the people who use it. Adding to the liveliness of this room is the fact that it's one of the more "public" rooms in the home, where we may host friends, neighbors and extended family.

The more we use the room, or the more activities that take place there, the more potential there is for clutter. Each hobby, sport and interest brings with it its own unique type of paraphernalia. However, we also want the room to be a relaxed, comfortable environment for lounging and socializing.

FUNCTION AND COMFORT
If a family member has a passion for crafts or a research-intensive hobby, you'll notice in the blink of an eye that related clutter builds up quickly and can make the living room less livable for others. Therefore, solutions and strategies that don't sacrifice function, style and comfort are essential when organizing the living room for use by everyone.

Before organizing anything, declutter every horizontal surface (floor, fireplace hearth, mantel, window ledges, piano, tabletops). Collect everything that doesn't belong (like spare change, phone chargers, cups and plates) and return these to their designated place (the articles on the other rooms in this book can help with this task).

Now turn your attention to what does belong. First consider what is actually being used on a regular basis. Things like headphones, a music stand, remote controls, hobby tools, sewing materials or kids' toys may all be used in the living room. Is there adequate storage for everything that you do not want visible? Consider installing an entertainment center, built-in bookcases or store-bought shelving. You might prefer more mobile options, such as decorative baskets or vintage luggage, or a mobile gaming cart.

Finally, make sure the living room reflects your current lifestyle and organizing goals. Is there a picture on the wall that you don't like? Are you holding on to unwanted gifts that will never be used? Honor meaningful items by discarding unloved ones. Instead of feeling ashamed or wasteful, be grateful for having an abundance of comforts and being able to share them through a donation center.

ZONES
When considering the layout of the room and the requisite furniture, think about the specific activities taking place there. Create a list of necessities for each activity and consider creating an area that allows that activity to function optimally. An area, or zone, is where several like items are grouped together for a specific type of activity or purpose. Living-room activity areas may include:

■ **Reading area** Requiring seating, lighting and a horizontal surface: a couch or chair; freestanding or table light; small side table big enough to hold a glass or cup, and maybe a box of bonbons.
■ **Entertaining area** Whether you have guests for morning coffee or an evening gathering, you might want a side table, game table, bar cart and games.

A BEAUTIFUL MIND
Every homeowner deserves a Zen-like area to revitalize, rejuvenate and read. Here, a purposefully small side table helps honor a zero clutter goal.

HIDE AND SLEEK
Make every inch count by utilizing drawers of various depths to stash headphones, yoga mats and movie-night blankets. Create multiple conversation zones by scattering upholstered pieces throughout the room wherever space permits. Try to avoid pushing furniture against the walls.

■ **Electronics area** Somewhere to keep the TV and games paraphernalia, such as DVDs, game controllers, remote controls, headphones, tablet or laptop. Perhaps a dedicated media unit with shelves for the devices and a drawer for the accoutrements is required, or simply dedicate a drawer or shelf in an existing piece of furniture to the accessories of our electronic age.

■ **Music area** A space for instruments, sheet music, music stands and amplifiers might also house your precious vinyl collection.

■ **Kids' space** You don't want the children's toys and games to take over your living space, but you can create a tidy zone within the room, with a storage system that the kids will use (see Toy Story, below).

TOY STORY

Having a bookcase or shelving unit in a room does not guarantee that your family's possessions will be more organized and less cluttered, which is why it's important to incorporate a system that works for everyone. Low-to-the-ground, open shelves allow children to help themselves to the toys of their choice. Regularly rotate toys and limit the number of them, so that cleanup time is quick and toy clutter is kept to a minimum.

Small toys for pets and toddlers and transparent, stackable shoe boxes are a match made in heaven. Use boxes that are not too deep to encourage one-toy-at-a-time retrieval, instead of emptying an entire toy chest to find a buried treasure.

Handheld game controllers fit nicely in canvas bins with handles, which are portable and slide on and off shelves like drawers. Create labels for each bin to identify the contents.

12 To have and to hold: living-room storage solutions

Within your room's zones, and based on the uses your living area has, you have a range of storage solutions available to you in a wide variety of materials and colors suited to any decor. These help to ensure everything stays categorized and organized. Some may even serve dual purposes. Here are some tips to help you choose.

1 Coffee tables
A coffee table with drawers or tiered shelves provides extra storage and lets you keep current reading materials organized and close at hand. A nest of tables is another idea: if you entertain a lot you will have enough surfaces when guests need them, but the system only takes up the room of one side table when not in use.

2 Chests and trunks
Ottomans (with lids), chests, trunks and cube-shaped boxes are perfect for stowing movie-night blankets or overnight guest linens. They can also be used as small tables.

3 Bags
Marbles, jacks, small game and puzzle pieces, decks of cards: keeping like-with-like items well organized is often a perplexing and puzzling problem for parents. Bags come in an infinite variety of sizes and shapes. Options include plastic ziplock sandwich bags, drawstring shoe bags, canvas tote bags, clothespin bags and cosmetic gift pouches. Bags are soft, fold easily and can be highly durable.

4 Lockers
Narrow, repurposed pieces can be angled into corners of the living room for extra storage. School lockers and old filing cabinets can provide interest.

5 Risers
Use these to increase visibility of items kept toward the back of a shelf.

6 Shelves
You have the choice of wall mounting shelves or purchasing one of the many freestanding bookshelf options. Be aware that store-bought bookcase shelves are usually 9–12 in. (23–30 cm) deep. When purchasing containers to be housed on shelves, measure the shelf and be sure to only buy what will fit.

7 Keeping shelves shipshape
Baskets, boxes and bins allow you to get full use of your shelf space, since you can use them to stow a variety of objects of differing shapes that would not normally sit neatly on a shelf. There are many good-looking options to choose from.

8 Stacked trays
A tower of trays is a great space-saving device and especially useful in living rooms that serve various purposes. Stack the trays, with their contents still in place, when not in use. Tray sets are no longer just office black but are made in many colors and materials to complement your decor. Decorate wooden trays, or look for ready-made systems that double as a side table when stacked.

9 Magazine files
Whether housed on shelves, a table or on the floor next to a chair, magazine files can keep notebooks, loose papers, magazines and slim books neatly standing straight up.

10 Binders
Storage binders with vinyl sleeves keep entertainment media accessible and they also save space. Plus, print options add a punch of color. Opt for binders with metal rings so the pages can be rearranged quickly. Label binders according to genre.

11 Silverware caddy
Repurpose this item to house reading glasses, remote controls, writing supplies and cellphones. The caddy can be easily carried to chairs or couches and then returned to the shelf. Again, these are available in many materials and colors.

12 Bookends and shelf dividers
These are both handy and decorative, used to spatially separate items on shelves.

MAINTAINING CLUTTER-FREE SURFACES

Having decluttered and organized your living room into a space that promotes wellbeing and happiness, it's important to be mindful of sticking to a maintenance plan. Order is more easily maintained if you don't allow clutter to creep back onto tabletops, piano benches, shelves or other horizontal surfaces. Here are some strategies for common clutter culprits:

❶ Receipts
Keep only what's necessary and trash the others. To contain the ones you need, a glass jar, a plastic bag, a poly envelope, a "spike stick" or a large mailing envelope all work, as would a shoe box or file folder.

❷ Magazine management
Limit your number of magazine and periodical subscriptions, and have a system for discarding the old as the new arrive. Save current issues in a magazine file on a shelf or in a magazine rack on the floor. Lifetime "keepers" can send the mags to a bookbinding service where they'll add hardcovers and spines so they can be kept upright on a bookshelf.

❸ Mail
Junk mail? Recycling bin. Regular mail? Place in designated cubby or basket.

❹ Coupons
Place these directly into your wallet or, if they are to be shared, put coupons in the administration station (see page 136).

❺ Newspapers
Keep a recycling bin for disposal of newspapers immediately after reading.

❻ Gift certificates
Enter the expiration date on the calendar and set a reminder on an electronic calendar one month in advance of that date. Keep the certificates in the administration station.

❼ Coins
Deposit spare change into a jar with a wide mouth, a cigar box, bowl, decorative mug or beer stein. When the container is three-quarters full, take it to the bank. Most banks now have counting machines that customers can use for free.

❽ Dirty dishes
Make a rule that everyone will deal with any dirty dishes anywhere in the house by the end of each day: and that doesn't mean just putting them in the kitchen, but washing, drying and putting them away, or putting them in the dishwasher.

❾ Toys
Make sure kids know they are responsible for picking up their own toys every evening.

SOLID OPTION
A heavy-duty table on wheels provides plenty of surface area for cocktails, coffee, or coloring books. Kick the habit of automatically renewing magazines and journals and remember to edit reading material three or four times a year.

ORGANIZING MEDIA

The world of movies, books, music and gaming has changed significantly over the past decade, as have the devices we use to enjoy them. While the digital age has its benefits, the average homeowner isn't yet 100 percent digital. Organize collections by subdividing each medium into subcategories.

I have laid out some suggestions here. Use what works for you and remember that your filing system is only as good as your ability to retrieve what you need, when it's needed.

BOOKS
These can be ordered on the shelf to your preferred specification, such as:
■ *Genre*—the category of the book, such as self-help, short story, humor, romance.
■ *Subject*—what/who the book is about, such as time travel, etiquette, Mick Jagger.
■ *Author*
■ *Color*
■ *Size*

The dos and don'ts of collectibles

Collections are as varied and as interesting as their owners. They can be worth a lot of money or a little, but that's not necessarily their value. They may have been collected over a lifetime or within minutes on an auction website, but if everything is considered a favorite, then nothing is truly special and unique. Keep only the things that are worth the cost or effort of properly and proudly displaying and maintaining. Consider the following when decluttering and managing treasures:

- **Don't** hang on to things hoping they will be valuable someday.
- **Don't** keep items just because they were given to you.
- **Don't** think that every piece of a bigger set needs to be acquired in order for a personal collection to be complete.
- **Do** keep collectibles that tell a personal story and bring joy.
- **Do** unify photos and hanging art by using frames of the same color.
- **Do** paint "gallery walls" in a neutral color.
- **Do** focus on texture and lighting in the area where collections are displayed.

MUSIC
Arranged in alphabetical order by performer is a good system, perhaps further categorized by musical genre, such as:
- *Country*
- *Hip-hop*
- *Holiday*
- *Jazz*
- *Rock*

DVDS
(and maybe even videos) Genre categorizing could accompany alphabetical organizing by title.
- *Adventure*
- *Children's*
- *Comedy*
- *Drama*
- *Family*
- *History*
- *Musical*
- *Romance*
- *Sci-fi*
- *Western*

GAMES
Genre categorizing could accompany alphabetical organizing by title.
- *Action*
- *Adventure*
- *Other:* music, puzzles, trivia, education
- *Sports*

FAVORITE PIECES
Keeping the clutter to a
minimum in the living room
allows you to better enjoy the
many uses this space can have,
but that does not mean you
have to do away with treasured
possessions or favorite prints,
photographs or works of art.
Pictures, ornaments and
accessories can be better shown
off in clutter-free areas.

Kitchen

A GOOD START
When arranging your utensils and food storage, be selfish but be consistent. Store like with like, but don't forget ease of use. Use the system illustrated here as a springboard for your own setup.

Not too long ago, the kitchen was used for one reason and one reason only: the preparation of meals. Today's kitchens, however, take center stage and often serve multiple purposes.

The kitchen has become the social hub of the home, where friends and family might gather before, during and after a meal. In addition, many of us use the kitchen as the family conference room; where we plan and synch our sports, work, academic and social calendars. Family members create art and science projects here, open the mail and pay the bills—all this between celebrating birthdays and holidays and enjoying sit-down, home-cooked meals or dining in on takeout food.

THE HEART OF THE HOME
The kitchen is the most public room in today's home. It's seen and used the most. Homeowners who crave organization often feel overwhelmed and aren't quite sure where or how to begin. The good news is that getting started is usually the most difficult part. Organizing the heart of the home takes CPR: Categorizing, Purging and Re-Zoning. Start by considering these common kitchen categories of clutter:

Double trouble Eliminate duplicates; keep only the best and most-used sports hydration bottles, vegetable peelers, vases or any other twins/triplets you've acquired.

Clutter from another Keep one container for items that migrated into the kitchen but belong elsewhere, such as hair ribbons, craft supplies, shoes, sporting equipment, homework and clothing. Save time and energy by returning all items to where they belong once a day.

Utility drawer items Banish battery and lightbulb supplies, spare change, cords and cables to the laundry/utility area or linen closet (see pages 60–65 and 106–109).

FINDING THE RIGHT RECIPE
Maintaining a well-organized, clutter-free kitchen in the 21st century is challenging. In addition to being the room where multiple activities take place, kitchens are "drop zones" filled with things we purchase or acquire: cooking gadgets, electronic gizmos, small appliances, coupons, backpacks, pet treats—you name it! The marketplace is filled with organizing products at every price point that promise to help us do things faster, better and more efficiently. So why is it we still can never find the right lid to a plastic container when we need it? Kitchens often take longer to organize than other rooms for several reasons.

■ A lot of different activities take place in the kitchen—not just cooking.
■ It's a "public" room in your home—used by everyone.
■ There are a lot places to stow things—countertops, cabinets, shelves and drawers.

When planning kitchen storage, the key is to dedicate each cabinet or drawer to a particular type of kitchen paraphernalia. The kitchen shown right is well appointed in terms of cupboard space: there is a place for everything and everything is in its place.

SURVEY YOUR SPACE
Transforming casa de chaos into casa de calm is not only about editing possessions and putting things into labeled containers. Before that happens, you need to analyze the space and figure out which storage solutions are the most appropriate, chosen from the many that are available to everyone, everywhere. The real challenge comes from working within the architectural parameters of your space.

Floor You can use the floor space between cabinets, refrigerator and stove, under shelves, anywhere that does not get

1 Cooking utensils used most often (can opener, cooking tongs, spatulas, spoons)

2 Canned foods, pasta, rice, bread, herbs, spices, vinegars, oils, cooking wines, baking ingredients, breadcrumbs

10 Cutlery drawer with sliding compartments for additional storage

3 Items rarely used (chafing dishes, fondue pots)

4 Mugs

5 Wine, bar and water glasses

6 Pots, pans, ovenproof baking dishes and larger pieces used while cooking (colander, steamer basket, cheese grater)—a divided drawer is an option.

7 Keep larger cooking utensils in an accessible drawer (whisks, measuring cups, spoons, pot-holders, trivets).

8 Store dish detergent, surface and oven cleaner, scouring pads, dishtowels and dishcloths under the sink.

9 Dishwasher

11 Dinner/salad/ dessert plates, bowls, everyday serving dishes—a divided drawer is an option.

12 Placemats, napkins, napkin rings, drink coasters

13 Baking sheets, baking pans, muffin tins—I highly recommend vertical dividers in this cabinet.

14 Larger appliances (food processor, rice cooker, crockpot, waffle iron)

Opposite side of the island
- Food wraps, foils, parchment paper, bags for lunches
- Mixing bowls, platters, trays, leftover food storage containers plus lids

underfoot, by finding boxes, bins and baskets that fit into the space.

Wall: shelves Extra shelves can fit into even the smallest wall spaces and still be useful for storage or display. Store lesser-used items on high shelves, and those you turn to often at a height within reach.

Wall: hanging storage Shoe-pocket bags, magnetic strips, rods, pegboards, cup hooks, shower curtain hooks, self-adhesive hooks; there are many options available for hanging items that can make great use of otherwise wasted space.

SUGAR AND SPICE, PASTA AND RICE: ORGANIZATION MAKES IT OH SO NICE

You can adapt the following guidelines within a kitchen that features several smaller cabinets rather than a single large pantry.

To declutter and organize a pantry, begin by removing everything and washing and drying the shelves and walls. As always, discard anything past its expiration date, and donate unopened cans and dry goods that you no longer want.

As you replace the items, be aware that having dedicated areas streamlines meal prep and shopping trips. At a glance, you'll know what needs replenishing.

THE COLD WAR: HOW TO ORGANIZE THE FRIDGE

The beauty of organizing the fridge is that questions regarding what stays and what goes are more easily answered than in other areas of the home.

The contents are either past their expiration date or still good, which determines what is kept and what is tossed. And, best of all, even the largest of fridges can be tidied and organized in just a few hours.

Clean and declutter the fridge in the same pattern as you'd read a book; start in the upper left corner and move to the right, from top to bottom. Remove everything from the shelves, drawers and doors. Trash anything past its due date, including leftovers, "barely-theres" and questionables. Clean the interior and replace items using a like-with-like system, similar to the one at right.

Make sure the fridge temperature is set to between 37 and 39°F (3 and 4°C), and aim to keep it full. A full fridge stays colder, but if you have more fridge than food you can top it up with gallons of water to keep it properly chilled.

To keep the refrigerator working to optimum efficiency, check and clean the door seals twice a year—if a dollar bill won't hold in place when you close the door on it, it's time to clean or replace the seals.

Door Condiments, cans, cartons, or bottles.

Upper shelves (1) Ready-to-eat foods, such as yogurt, cheese and dairy.

Middle shelves (2) Typically where leftovers and other cooked foods are kept; however, fresh produce in plain sight encourages healthy snacking.

Drawers (3) Separate fruits and veggies. Do not refrigerate onions, potatoes, garlic, acorn squash or winter squash.

Lower (4) Meats, shellfish and poultry should be kept on the lowest shelves or in the lowest drawers to avoid drips that might contaminate other foods. Thaw items in washable containers.

10 Top tips for kitchen organization

Accepting the architectural parameters of your kitchen—the things you can't change—these tips will make what you have work better.

1 Invest and nest
Invest in nesting containers that are microwave, dishwasher and freezer safe. Look for lids that snap to the base of the containers and remain neatly stacked, taking up minimum space.

2 Rolling along
A rolling cart with locking rubber-rimmed casters lets you slice and dice safely without worrying about the cart wandering. Once finished, the cart can be returned to a storage location, thus freeing up kitchen floor space.

3 Customize zones
Keep things in zones where they'll be used. If you typically use certain spices when cooking, place those spices within easy reach of the stove.

4 Console table
When countertop space is sparse, a slim console table can work as an alternative to an island. It could also provide surface space for canisters, a beverage station or small appliances. Open shelves below keep wine or baskets of produce within arm's reach.

5 Spin, stack, cube
Turntables, expandable tiered shelves and wine-cubby storage-like spaces allow multiple items to be stashed and stored, yet remain visible and easily accessible.

6 Push, pull, glide
Pull-out shelving is the ultimate solution, but it isn't an affordable option for everyone. Rectangular-shaped containers, all the better if see-through, serve the same purpose—they pull out easily and contain produce and packets for visibility and accessibility. If it isn't visible or easy to reach, it's less likely to be used.

7 Deep drawers
Dedicate a deep drawer near your cooking zone for storing extra oils, foils and wraps or baking sheets.

8 Magnetic attraction
A magnetic knife strip uses vertical space, keeps knives from getting dull and frees up precious counter space.

9 Vertical is visible
Pots, pans, cooking utensils and pot holders may be hung vertically if horizontal space is at a premium. There are racks, rods and a variety of hooks available for hanging items. Things that are stored vertically are easy to see and get used more often.

10 Drawer war
Use adjustable dividers to separate and organize things within drawers.

4 Clever cabinets

Replacing existing kitchen cabinets is an expensive proposition, so if you are looking for more storage space, consider how best to make the most of what you already have.

1 Pull a fast one: blind corners
Use every inch of hard-to-access corner cabinets by installing hinged organizers on full extension slides, with wire racks, for right or left corner cabinets.

2 Doors
Top-hinge cabinet doors never bump and bang into each other and can be a great choice for anyone who finds themself dodging cabinet doors in awkward positions.

3 Tray stay
Lower-level (base) cabinets often don't provide vertical storage space for pizza pans, cookie sheets, cutting boards, baking pans, muffin tins and cooling racks. This can be quickly fixed by installing a slotted divider created to fit inside cabinets and keep trays on their side, making it easy to grab just one.

4 Kicking it up a notch
When cabinets are sparse, convert a base cabinet's toe-kick into a shallow rollout. This space can be perfect for pot lids, cookie sheets, serving platters, plastic storage, grilling tools, food wraps or place mats and tablecloths.

Kitchen pantries provide storage for items used most often. You could designate sections on pantry shelves for the following areas:

- Baking supplies
- Beverages
- Breads, buns, biscuits for sandwich making
- Breakfast items: cereal, oatmeal
- Crackers, cookies, chips, snacks
- Canned goods: vegetables, fruits, meats, fish, soups and broths
- Dried fruits, nuts, seeds
- Dry goods: beans, grains, rice, pasta
- Jam, jelly, nut butters
- Oils, vinegars, sauces, syrups, honey
- Seasonings
- Spices

Optional
- Disposable picnic products: paper plates, cups, straws, condiment packets
- Wraps, foils, sandwich bags
- Paper towels, paper napkins

CLEARLY CORRALLED
Store pantry staples like pastas, grains, nuts and seeds in glass jars to make them easy to find. With just one glance, you know when it's time to restock.

NO PANTRY, NO PROBLEM
Convert an armoire-style storage cabinet into a pantry. Custom fit with deep drawers for canisters of sugars, flours, grains and pastas. Rest heavy serving platters safely in the bottom drawer, and display pretty crocks on top. Narrow shelves on doors hold sauces, spices and oils.

13 Top tips for a clutter-free pantry

A strategically stocked pantry makes meal planning and preparation quicker and less stressful. Try these tips for organizing the pantry.

1 Food and food-related products only

Refrain from putting unrelated items in the pantry, such as giftwrap, memorabilia and electronics.

2 Edit cookbook collections

If a Thai cookbook has been sitting unused for 11 years, let it go; remember it's okay to do this, even if it was a gift or signed by the author.

3 Transparency is key

See-through, stackable containers with tight-fitting lids (or vacuum sealing) are great for holding dry goods. By using transparent containers, there's no need to label the obvious.

4 Bookends
Use bookends or shelf dividers to keep cookbooks vertical.

5 Clearly label doppelgangers
For example, look-alike types of flour: self-rising, all-purpose, cake flour.

6 Keep it angled
If space is at a premium, remember that round containers waste space—so if it's tight, use square or rectangle containers.

7 Snacks
Stock a basket or box in an area that children can access with self-serve snacks such as applesauce cups, granola bars, fruit chews, pretzels and nuts.

8 Beverage-can dispensers
If you buy drink cans in bulk, a dispenser will keep them accessible and not taking up too much room, whether in the pantry or fridge.

9 Know when it runs out
Decant big-box, bulk purchases into large, transparent containers, making it easy to see how much of an item remains. This reduces duplicate purchases and the number of giant boxes in the pantry.

10 Over the door
Use the space behind the pantry door by installing a back-of-door shelf system.

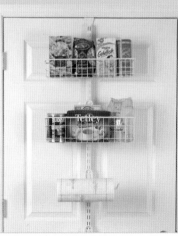

11 Shelf labels
Labels on shelves help reinforce maintenance habits; the goal is to have everyone in the family return items where they belong. Labels confirm and clarify where everything belongs.

12 Fine mesh
Wire-mesh baskets can be washed and dried more quickly than solid plastic or acrylic boxes, which might make them an attractive proposition.

13 Pick me up
Wire tier risers provide extra vertical space and keep labels visible and items easy to reach.

WHEN IT COMES TO THE DRAWER WAR: LESS IS MORE

Buy more, use less. That's what clients tell me happens when they shop for kitchen do-dads. As a result, kitchen drawers become densely packed and disorganized. It's easy to get carried away when acquiring kitchen gadgets, because bells and whistles promise to improve our culinary experiences. While shopping we become overwhelmed. We want to select the perfect cutting board so we end up buying several: wood, plastic and silicone. Then, typically, we end up using one favorite while the others are ignored.

To declutter those drawers you need to decide which kitchen essentials are personal must-haves, bearing in mind that no two lists will be the same, since every cook and every kitchen is unique. Below are a few ideas to help determine what's important enough to keep or newly acquire and what's not being used and should be cleared out.

■ **Basic kitchen starter kit** This is my suggestion as the absolute basic requirements: can opener; bottle opener; tongs; wire whisk; ladle; wooden spoon; flipper; sieve; cutting board; vegetable scrubber; hot pads, some of which double as a jar opener.
■ **Not-so-basic kitchen tools** You may need these extras also: rubber spatula; grater; pastry blender; rolling pin; potato masher.

TOOLS YOU USE
Knowing what a tool is best used for is the only way for you to decide whether you need it or not. If you cook spaghetti often, then by all means keep a spaghetti server in your toolkit.

■ **Thermometers** With the freezer, the fridge and meat, a few degrees can mean the difference between being unsafe and safe. The only way to know for sure is to take an accurate reading of the temperature of the freezer, the fridge and roasted, grilled or cooked meats. Bakers should add a candy thermometer.
■ **Knives** Instead of buying a set of knives, pick and choose those you're most likely to use regularly. A chef's knife, paring knife, serrated knife and boning knife are adequate for most home cooks. A carving knife and kitchen shears (that come apart for cleaning) are useful, too.
■ **Measuring cups and spoons** Serious bakers and cooks measure ingredients on a food scale, but for most of us following American recipes, measuring cups and spoons are the norm. You need one set of spoons and one of cups. Choice of material—glass, silicone, ceramic, plastic or stainless steel—is a matter of personal preference, as is handle length and whether they are spouted or not.
■ **Strainer** There are three types of strainers to consider: mesh for smooth sauces and sifting flour; large hole (also known as colander) for pasta and veggies; and a strainer with holes small enough to drain rice or orzo.
■ **Mixing bowls** The goal is to avoid mixing bowls that tend to warp, dent, chip, stain or absorb odors, as well as ones that are too heavy or have too-high or too-low sides. A nice

pouring spout, skidproof bottoms and fitted lids are other options to consider.

Peeler Two types of produce peelers are commonly found in kitchen drawers: the Y-shaped peeler and the linear (straight) peeler. Think about whether you prefer peeling toward or away from your body and consider the produce being peeled. Big and round items like potatoes and apples do better with a Y-peeler; skinny and long foods like carrots and cucumbers do better with a linear peeler.

SPATULAS WORTH FLIPPING OVER

Spatulas (also called flippers or turners) are the second-most reached-for utensil in my kitchen (knives are first). Because there are a variety of spatulas to choose from, it's important to inventory spatulas and their various uses, including folding, turning, flipping and lifting.

■ **Fish spatula** This is easily my very favorite kitchen utensil! Used for lifting delicate, crispy cookies off a warm cookie sheet, cradling and draining slippery fried and poached eggs and gently flipping flaky fish fillets (thus the name), it's the go-to spatula. The best ones are agile, have a honed, slanted edge curving upward, and are made of metal—meaning they should not be used on nonstick cookware.

■ **One-material silicone spatula** Made without a wooden or nylon handle, there are no crevices, which means there is no bacteria buildup. Plus, one-material, one-piece, means

the spatula head will never pop off. And they are completely dishwasher safe.

■ **Metal spatula** For flipping heavy burgers, cutting into dense brownies or turning pancakes.

■ **Spatula-spoon** This useful tool resembles a nearly flattened spoon. It is useful for stirring heavy foods like chili or stew and breaking up ground beef or sausage while browning. The spatula-spoon's straight end provides full contact with a flat surface.

■ **Offset spatula** Also known as a frosting or icing spatula, this metal tool is perfect for spreading peanut butter, mayonnaise or mustard, and for gently lifting very small portions or very hot baked goods without burning one's fingers or messing up the entire pan of treats.

> 66 Kitchens are used for much more than cooking. Start organizing your kitchen by creating a designated 'zone' for every activity and store the tools or supplies you'll need nearby. 99

Dining spaces

When a client contacts me about getting their entire home organized, and I hear the slightest bit of frustration or fear in their voice, I ask why? More than likely, the reason is that they feel overwhelmed and don't know where to begin. If the home has a dedicated dining area, this is where I recommend they start.

The first reason is that, generally speaking, it is faster and easier to organize a rarely used room than one that is occupied night and day by several members of the family. Secondly, with a few exceptions, the items in this room aren't as emotionally provocative as those found elsewhere in the home.

YOUR STYLE

Keep in mind that life is expressed in small details throughout the home. The dining area is where I encourage you to show off, even when dining simply *en famille*. Think of the dining area as the place where the details of organizing and decorating give the home a soul. Things displayed in this area are the frosting on the cake and special attention should be given to each detail, especially when creating a formal area.

Begin by analyzing your personal preference regarding abundance or restraint. Organizing isn't about throwing things away needlessly. The goal of decluttering is to figure out what's wanted, needed, useful and appreciated. The items we keep tell a story about us and the best stories have good guys and bad guys. When organizing and decluttering, the goal is to keep the good guys and get rid of as many useless bad guys as possible.

FOR STARTERS

In the same way that meals aren't just about satisfying hunger, dining is not only about food; it's about creating an ambience. The dining area needs to be a feast for the senses. It should feel, look and smell as good as the meal tastes, and it should be your idea of tastefully appointed. But that doesn't give you licence to keep a million complicated embellishments.

Dining rooms are often buried in "transfer clutter." These objects have no business being there, but were transferred there during the decluttering of another, more regularly occupied room. Or, the clutter has made it here because you don't know where else to put it. For example, "Here's a pair of pants I ordered online. They don't fit and need to be returned. I'll print a label, take it to FedEx later, but I'll just leave it here for now." Unfortunately, "later" never happens. You need to clear the transfer clutter and prevent it from returning.

Begin by decluttering everything on and around the dining table and chairs. Once things have been removed from the tabletop and chairs, prevent clutter from accumulating again by setting the table. Perhaps put out a few dishes, glasses and silverware, or a tablecloth or runner and a bowl of fruit or vase of flowers. There's no need to create an excessively styled and propped table. Instead, keep in mind that a simple thing, done well, is beautiful.

IT HAS ITS USES

One of life's greatest pleasures is surrounding yourself with things you love. However, you can have too much of a good thing, and the dining area needs to be a mix

ALL WHITE IS ALL RIGHT
Family-friendly surfaces that easily wipe clean look hygienic and help simplify housekeeping routines. Placing a vase on the table, or laying it with just a few items, will encourage everyone to keep it clutter free.

ASK YOURSELF

While sorting and categorizing, everyone appreciates a little motivation, education and inspiration. To help you figure out which dining accessories you need, love or can do without, answer these questions:

Does this item represent your current tastes?

When was the last time you hosted a fondue party or used place cards? This is where the phrase "use it or lose it" should become your decluttering mantra.

Does looking at, using it or owning it make you deliriously happy?

If the candelabra you were given as a wedding present is ornate and hideous and drips wax on the tablecloth, why keep it? A present doesn't have to be present in your life forever. Gift yourself by letting go of things that aren't contributing to your goal of a clutter-free home.

Are you holding on to it hoping to pass it down to one of your children?

If so, has the child expressed an interest in it, or are you "forcing" an inheritance? The fragile, formal dinnerware that once belonged to your granny is not a good fit for your city-dwelling daughter's modern, studio-apartment lifestyle.

Doubles are troubles! Do you have another or very similar item?

If so, how many do you really need? Only florists are required to keep dozens of vases; keep a few unique vases—or item in question—of varying dimensions and shapes, then let the rest go.

Would you rebuy that same item today if the current one disappeared?

The mammoth tulipiere you bought during a tulip tour in Holland has remained flower free on the sideboard for years. It cost a small fortune, but keeping it doesn't bring back money spent. It's perfectly okay to admit mistakes. Lesson learned: move on, and let it go.

DINE IN AND TAKE OUT
If you are short on space, consider expanding dining options with a built-in, pull-out feature. A surface used as an office space during the day can double as a cozy table for two after hours.

of beauty and practicality. The pleasure of eating in a well-organized space is undeniable.

Does the dining area make you glad to be eating at home? If not, work at making it inviting, comfortable and easy to maintain. If there's a hutch or sideboard in the room, pull out each and every item. Sort items into categories and inspect and analyze everything with the eye of a museum curator. Create a rule that you will start using everything you own. No more saving items for special occasions. If, among your decluttering finds, you rediscover long-forgotten giant goblets, use them for hot chocolate with whipped cream. Breaking with tradition can infuse energy and life into your possessions because by doing so you will actually be using them. Replace confusion with confidence, and let the way you use items reflect your individual personality and lifestyle.

Throw out chipped glasses and get rid of high-maintenance items, like silver that needs polishing, and tablecloths that need ironing.

THE DISH ON DISHES

Do you own dishes that are never used but supposedly kept for special occasions? Reasons for not using these dishes include:

- They are not food-safe.
- They cannot be used in the microwave.
- They are not dishwasher-safe.
- They are too formal for everyday dining.
- They are stored in a hard-to-access-place.
- They are fragile and chip or break easily.

If any of these reasons rings true for you, consider donating or consigning the special dishes, as well as your everyday dishes, and replacing them with one set of durable, neutral-

OPEN SHELVES
When everything is out in the open and on display, order and minimalism are easily maintained.

5 Storage of dining essentials

You have established what you need and don't need, now here are some tips for organizing and protecting your dining and entertaining accoutrements.

1 Wire racks
Increase storage space by adding wire racks to the bottom of shelves. Depending on your requirements, you can stack items without damaging them, or even hang stemware.

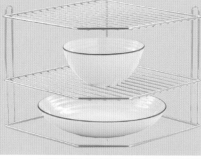

2 Dividers
Use dividers in drawers to sort items by type so that they are quick and easy to retrieve, including the little things, such as pebbles for vases, tealights, napkin rings and wine-glass charms.

3 Stop the clock
Over time, silver naturally tarnishes. To slow the oxidation process, make sure silver is double-wrapped in both a cloth bag and a Mylar or polyethylene bag. Sticks of ordinary white chalk help absorb moisture and delay oxidation, too.

4 Padded safety
If the decision to keep more than one set of china is firm, store the special-occasion set in padded storage bags with labels.

5 China on shelves
To reduce the chance of chipping when china is stored on a shelf, place paper plates, coffee filters or felt protectors between plates and refrain from stacking cups and saucers. Invert the lids of china sugar bowls, creamers, teapots or soup tureens and keep a piece of felt between the lid and the base unit.

colored crockery that transcends both formal and informal uses.

MEASURING UP
Furniture that is disproportionate in size to the room can make a space feel cramped and uncomfortable. If you have decluttered your dining area but it still does not feel right, perhaps the furniture needs to be bettter positioned, thinned out or replaced with appropriately sized items.

- **Table** The table is the room's centerpiece. Analyze its shape and size to make sure it is scaled to the room. Allow about 3 ft (1 m) of space between the walls and the dining chairs, when pushed away from the table. Anything less might indicate that a smaller dining table would be appropriate.
- **Rug** A dining room rug should extend about 16 in. (40 cm) beyond the back legs of the chairs when the chairs are under the table. You can, of course, have a bigger rug, but aim to leave 6 in. (15 cm) of bare floor around it. Remember that a rug under a table will meet with food and drink spills, so choose wisely.
- **Elbow room** Bear in mind that each diner needs about 24 in. (60 cm) of table space to avoid rubbing elbows when eating.
- **Sideboard** Buffets or sideboards should be deep enough to hold your largest serving platter. If on surveying the items you want stored in the sideboard you think you need it deeper, remember that, like the table size, you need a space of about 3 ft (1 m) between chair and sideboard when the chair is pulled out.
- **Central light** If a hanging light fixture or chandelier is positioned above the table, it should dangle no less than 3 ft (1 m) above the tabletop, so that is does not encroach on your space.
- **Centerpiece** Keep centerpieces about 12 in. (30 cm) tall and no taller than 16 in. (40 cm) to allow guests to see each other when seated.

1 If placing art on a wall above the sideboard, the space will look most comfortable if the painting is centered above the furniture.

2 With a chair pulled out, you need 3 ft (1 m) of space between it and the wall or next piece of furniture.

3 Each diner needs about 24 in. (60 cm) of table space to avoid rubbing elbows when eating.

4 If you have a rug, make sure its size is adequate to allow for chair movement.

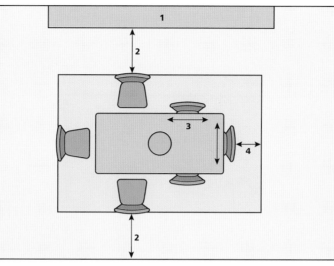

EVERYTHING'S HERE
What once was a formal dining room is now a colorful, family-friendly place to share meals; bookshelves contain cookbooks, and around the banquette are the glasses and dining accessories that are regularly used.

LIGHT FOR SPACE

Lighting is especially important in dining areas and can make them feel more spacious. Having a variety of light sources creates a warm glow that adds to the ambience. Candles and candlestick holders, mirrored wall sconces, hurricane lanterns, buffet lamps and chandeliers help illuminate a room. The more sources of light you have at your disposal, the more options you have to create the right atmosphere.

THE BUTLER'S PANTRY

If you are lucky enough to live in an older home with a butler's pantry, it needs to be decluttered like the rest of the house. Butler's pantries vary from elaborate, with a wine fridge, sink, ice, numerous cupboards and drawers to spare, to only a countertop, a couple drawers and maybe a cupboard.

Whatever the size, the same organizing and decluttering rules apply.

PURPOSEFULLY REPURPOSING

Not everyone who has a separate dining room uses it. The typical family entertains much less than in years gone by, and spends more time eating out. In addition, "open concept" homes are becoming the norm. In these, the living room blends into the dining room, into the kitchen and into family room, such that all of a family's activities occur in one oversized room.

If you find that your dining room sits unused for much of the year, grant yourself permission to break tradition by converting it into a room that will be used more often for a different purpose—perhaps as a playroom, home gym or home office, or a practical space where kids complete projects and homework, and adults enjoy hobbies.

You can retain the dining furniture—so it's there if you need it for a big family Christmas or Thanksgiving meal—but repurpose its uses. For example, a china hutch doesn't have to hold china. It's perfect storage for office supplies, quilting fabrics or genealogy research. Just remember that it's okay to use each room in a way that makes sense to you and your lifestyle needs. An underused dining space has no energy, whereas a room that is lived in and utilized, regardless of the purpose for which it was originally intended, brings contentment to the family.

HAPPY-HOUR HOW-TO: SETTING UP A BAR

Refer to this list when stocking and setting up your own bar, whether on an elegant bar cart, or the top of your dining-room sideboard. You won't need everything detailed here, but consider the drinks you will be serving and choose the items from the list as required.

Toolkit
Corkscrew, bottle opener, shaker, cutting board, jigger, paring knife, citrus juicer, zester, muddler, toothpicks, cocktail napkins, ice bucket, tongs.

Mixers
Tonic, club soda, sparkling water, fruit juices, soft drinks.

Garnish
Celery, lemon, lime, olives, salt, sugar.

Liquor
Vodka, gin, rum, tequila, whiskey, scotch.
Beer, wine, liqueurs, ports. The most popular vary, depending on a wide variety of factors, including age group and budget.

Small plates for hors d'oeuvres
Usually 6 in. (15 cm) or smaller for cocktail nibbles.

Glasses
Knowledge of which drink belongs in which glass is something that bartenders pride themselves on. However, since most of us don't have bartender skills or storage space for such a wide variety of oddly shaped and sized glasses, confidently use whatever you have or consider renting glasses for special occasions.

Laundry room

The laundry room is easily one of the hardest-working rooms in the house, despite the fact that it may not even be a room at all! Many washers and dryers are located in a closet, garage or basement instead of a separate space dedicated to cleaning clothes.

Thankfully, only the barest essentials are required to do laundry—electricity, water, a washer, properly vented dryer or clothesline, and vent. However, many of us own a lot more garments, sheets and towels than our grandparents owned, and while we wear our stuff less, we tend to launder it more.

Historically, the washing tools and cleaning agents used depended on a variety of factors, including location, weather and fabrics. Many paintings depict stones and sticks, known as wash bats, being used to clean the sturdy cotton clothing of Eastern Europe and Asia, while gentler methods, such as washboards, were used on the more delicate fabrics of Western European garments. Clothespins weren't invented until the 18th century, so clothes dried on the grass, rocks, shrubs or trees. In larger houses, wooden frames on ropes were used during inclement weather to dry clothes indoors. Not surprisingly, laundry was done less frequently then than now.

While doing laundry today is practically effortless, it is still not a chore we look forward to. Thankfully, we have modern conveniences and reasonably priced products doing most of the hard work. However, it is still essential to create a sustainable laundry routine and an orderly laundry area to minimize the tasks at hand. Consider and address the following points when organizing your laundry room:

Who
- does the laundry? Every man for himself? Or is one person in charge?
- does the ironing?
- puts the clean clothes away?

What
- other purpose does the laundry area serve? A utility closet, maybe? A pantry?
- else needs to be stored there? Iron and ironing board? Cleaning supplies?
- doesn't have a home? Pocket change? Stray buttons? Shoe polish?
- helpful items could be kept in the laundry area? A sewing kit or lint brush, perhaps?

When
- is the laundry done? A specific day? As the hamper fills? Or on demand, perhaps a uniform worn every day?
- are the prime times for washing, drying, folding and putting away? Multitasking is your friend. Throw in a load while cooking dinner and wait until morning to fold it and put it away, if that works best for you.
- are the dryer's lint filter and vent cleaned?

Where
- is the dirty laundry sorted?
- are the stained items soaked or treated?
- are delicates laundered and hung to dry?
- is the clean laundry folded?
- are clothes ironed?

Answer these questions and you will be well on your way to understanding how your laundry room should be organized to best benefit your family and your routine.

1 Repositionable floor-to-ceiling wire shelves make the most of vertical space, including corners.

2 Open shelving puts frequently used items within arm's reach.

3 Deep woven baskets of different sizes prevent stacks of folded items tumbling over.

4 High shelves store dangerous household cleaners safely out of the reach of children.

5 Extra laundry supplies can be stored behind closed doors.

6 A hanging rod with sturdy hangers allows damp items to dry completely.

7 Large clothing hampers make it easy for family members to deliver dirty sheets, towels and clothing on wash day.

SORTING IT OUT: ONE LOAD AT A TIME
A decluttered laundry area makes this household chore more bearable. Avoid wasting valuable space by limiting the number of cleaning products you purchase.

STOP CLUTTER BEFORE IT GETS THERE

The laundry room can so easily become the junk drawer of the house, with odds and ends and all sorts of unrelated items settling here, gathering into deep, sedimentary layers that sit untouched for years. You can avoid this piling up of clutter by understanding and addressing the reasons why it typically happens.

■ **Gotta have it** Items that people claim they can't throw away or give away. For example, a homeowner may have purchased an expensive steam iron but never used it. They remember needing it once and not having it, so now won't part with it for fear they might need it again. Remember the decluttering code of "uns" (see page 15). It's okay to donate something that is unused.

■ **Missing in action** Items hastily thrown into a "doorbell dread" container. Have you ever frantically filled a laundry basket with countertop clutter before answering the door to greet unexpected guests? Later, when the guests are gone and the item is needed, it's not where it belongs. Proper storage is about creating a home for something, so that minimal effort is required to find it and to put it away. Use the lessons learned in this book to streamline your possessions and give everything a home. Make "doorbell dread" a thing of the past.

■ **Address unknown** Items that don't have a designated "resting place" when not in use. Just like we have a street address and know exactly where we live, our things need a specific location where they live.

8 Bright ideas for organizing the laundry/utility area

Organizing the laundry area and all its accoutrements will help you combat clutter. These practical tips will help you keep your utility space in order, as well as ensuring that it is a more pleasant place to visit and safe for young ones.

1 Damp
Keep in mind factors such as moisture and dirt when assigning homes to cleaning equipment: hanging a wet mop in a closet with no ventilation is going to result in a smelly mop. Store bucket, mop and damp sponges on a water-resistant surface while they dry.

2 Within reach
Sturdy boxes or canvas bags for towels and rags need to be easily accessible for younger, smaller members of the family so that they can wipe up spills and participate in age-appropriate cleaning tasks.

3 Organized supplies
There are many ways to organize cleaning supplies. One way that saves trips back and forth is to designate containers for each of the areas that need to be cleaned—for example, one basket of cleaning supplies for bathrooms, one for kitchens and one for bedrooms.

4 Power
An electrical outlet is a must-have for charging the handheld cordless vacuum cleaner and rechargeable flashlight.

5 Expiration date
Install a shelf for extra lightbulbs, batteries and furnace filters. On new furnace filters, write dates when they need to be changed, and add a reminder on your calendar. Or pick an easy-to-remember date. I change mine when quarterly taxes are due.

6 Easy access
Bins for cleaners, polishes, oils and detergents should be easy to wipe clean and slide out from shelves without toppling other products.

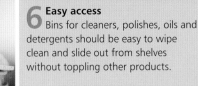

7 Recycling batteries
A large, wide-mouth glass container, such as a pickle jar, is perfect for housing expired or leaky batteries. Many office-supply stores allow customers to drop off batteries for recycling.

8 Hang it
Hang the broom, feather duster, dustpan and mop so that they won't fall over and become tripping hazards.

" Proper storage is about creating a home for something so that minimal effort is required to find it and to put it away. "

Before buying anything, think about how often it will be used and the most appropriate place to keep it. If the fancy garment steamer is bulky and doesn't fit in the utility closet or laundry room, it will end up cluttering another room and not being used.

LOOK AFTER THE DOLLARS

I need to come clean about decluttering and organizing the laundry room. I disagree with much of the advice given by traditional "experts." Yes, decanting detergents into decorative jugs will make the laundry room look nicer, but if you don't have the time, don't bother. If you struggle to hoist and pour detergent from bulky, economy-size bottles, simply buy smaller bottles. Why waste time and money buying extra containers and transferring and refilling products? Life isn't about having a picture-perfect home. If photographers are lining up to do a photo shoot in your laundry room, let them bring their own canisters.

My mantra: Save time, save money, save room. Why buy brand-new containers to stash an overabundance of stuff that should be recycled or trashed? Pretty containers are nice to look at, but most of the time the average laundry room is in dire need of a clutterectomy, not more containers. They are only useful if they serve a practical purpose efficiently. There is more than one way to store items. Look through the recycling bin in your kitchen and wash, then reuse containers from consumables, such as tins from cocoa, jars from condiments and jams, and wide-mouth bottles from ready-to-drink tea and juices.

SORTING IT OUT
Color-coded laundry baskets with handles make it easy for everyone to find what they need and put it back when finished. A single type of container, in a variety of colors, is the little secret to success.

9 Typical laundry challenges

Here are some ideas that will help you to complete tasks and tackle challenges that are typically faced in the laundry/utility area.

1 Soaking and pretreating stains
If the laundry room has no sink, keep a plastic dishpan under the kitchen or bathroom sink for soaking and pretreating stains. Use it to transport wet garments to the laundry room without a trail of drips.

2 Stash of trash
Have a small trash container in the laundry area for dryer lint, used dryer sheets and trash from pockets.

3 Organizing home-maintenance items
Designate sections on shelves for vacuum-cleaner bags, lightbulbs, air filters and batteries.

4 Drying a sweater
Sweaters can take a long time to dry if laid on a flat surface when hanging them is not an option. Use a pop-up mesh drying screen to minimize drying time and maximize air flow.

5 Getting it hot off the press
Wall-mounted ironing boards can be recessed behind a cabinet door or surface mounted against a wall and folded down when needed. You could also mount a freestanding ironing board on a wall rack for storage, or on a back-of-the-door mount.

6 MIAS—mending, ironing, alterations, stains
Create labels and place them directly on hangers with garments, indicating what needs to be done. For example, the hanger labeled "Mending" would hang a shirt that has a note on it reading, "Right sleeve, cuff, bottom button is missing."

7 Reducing ironing
Install a hanging rod with hangers on which to hang jackets and shirts fresh from the washer or dryer to keep garments wrinkle free. Immediately "snapping" and then folding clothes while they are warm reduces wrinkles, too.

8 Matchmaking strays and singles
Clothespins on a board or clothesline hold socks that are single but looking for their "sole" mates.

9 Unsolved mysteries
Designate a lost-and-found tote bag, where family members can claim missing items, such as things forgotten in pockets.

Kids' spaces

Nurseries for babies and toddlers, and rooms for tweens and teens need flexible storage solutions that can change as quickly as the kids who use them. Thankfully, options for organizing are plentiful, colorful and creative.

DISCARD AND DECIDE

The good news about organizing kids' rooms is that only two actions are required: discarding and deciding. Discarding should be easy: get rid of things kids no longer use by donating, consigning or trashing. Deciding is a little trickier, since an item you have decided to keep requires a second decision: Where is its home?

It is possible that, since you are reading this part of the book, your children have more toys and clothes than they need. More than they want. More than they will ever play with. Having too much of anything results in chaos, confusion and clutter. Decluttering, on the other hand, leads to creativity and contentment.

Begin by analyzing each child's needs. As children grow, their bedrooms and closets, as well as what's being stored in each, change (see Ages and Stages of Activity, page 72). Young children need an accessible area that makes tidying clothes and toys quick and easy. As they grow, more space for play might be required. A loft bed will maximize floor space, allowing for an under-the-bunk dollhouse or toy train track. Tweens may want a twin-sized daybed and trundle for sleepover guests.

Decide whether the bedrooms will be quiet zones where only sleep, rest and reading take place. If so, toys and games should be kept somewhere else, if possible. Homes without the option of a separate playroom or basement however, must make room in the bedroom.

TAMING THE TOY BOX

The first step in taming the toy box is to ascertain which items are worth keeping and storing. Parents tend to save sentimental items,

HIDE AND SEEK
Wooden boxes on wheels store stuffed animals, sleeping bags and board games. As the kids grow, the contents of their storage containers will change, but a fresh coat of paint will keep them relevant for many years to come.

4 Helping out

These four simple ideas mean that no one, no matter what their age, has an excuse not to help with the chores.

1 Bed head
Make it easy for young children to make the bed by keeping the bedding simple: don't complicate matters with top sheets or blankets. Use only a fitted sheet and comforter.

2 Dirty laundry
Place a hamper or laundry basket in each child's closet or bedroom. Even little ones can be taught that everything has a place.

3 Not quite dirty enough
Fix hooks or position a coat rack near laundry hampers to encourage kids of all ages to hang bath towels, pajamas and clothes that can be worn a second time without laundering.

4 Do it yourself
Foster independence by putting a stepstool in every closet until kids can reach the top shelves without assistance.

USE THE SPACE
In a shared bedroom (above), storage solutions can be painted differently for each child, giving each a sense of individuality.

STYLISH PAD
A streamlined room provides useful spaces to work and chill out (above right). As kids mature and sleepover guests become more frequent, a sofa that doubles as a bed might be a useful addition to the room. Make use of high shelving to ensure no storage space is lost.

even when kids are okay with moving on. When your child says they're ready to say goodbye to a stuffed animal, even if it's your favorite, give them the choice and your permission to let it go. Parents can teach kids the power of getting rid of things by letting them decide what goes. More often than not, a child is willing to let something go before the parent is. Young children want to please parents, but they get confused when they hear mixed messages. Statements like, "Oh, keep that; it's from Gran," make it sound as if things matter more than relationships. Gifts don't have to be retained for life: you can still love the giver, even if you don't love the gift.

STORING TOYS
As with much of the advice given in this book, when it comes to storing toys, keep it simple. A complicated system that separates toys into

very specific categorizes will overwhelm the child, who may prefer not to put a toy away for fear they might put it in the wrong place. Equally, setting up a system that keeps action figures in a different place to Barbies, and trains from one set separate to those from another brand, creates unnecessary work and slows down tidying-up time. Instead, keep categories broad—soft toys, dolls, Lego—and have boxes, bins or hampers that the toys can easily be "thrown" into and rummaged around in.

HANDLING HAND-ME-DOWNS
To get a handle on clothes as children grow, edit them every time the laundry is done. Why wait for a seasonal change to weed out too-short pants or a too-tight shirt? Every wash load is an opportunity for a "pitch-it" party, where clothes can be permanently removed from circulation.

66 Having too
much of anything
results in chaos,
confusion and
clutter. 99

Toss items that no longer fit into an outbound box near the washer, so that they don't unnecessarily take up drawer and closet space in the child's room. Then, have a seasonal clean-out day when items in the outbound box are given the "discard" or "decide" treatment and either donated or stored for the next in line. Children can do their bit, too. Add a "no-questions-asked" donation container in a hall closet, or near the laundry hamper, where everyone can put clothes that no longer fit or aren't being worn. When your son is handed a T-shirt in his least favorite color and says, "No way am I wearing that," he has a place to put the shirt, no questions asked.

THE 4 S'S OF STORING CLOTHES

When you have decided to keep items of clothing for future use, consideration should be given to how best to store them. The four S's are key to going from overflowing and overwhelmed to organized.

- **Size** If you have a large family, the clothes you keep for passing on may encompass a wide range of sizes. In this instance, size matters, and it can be a good idea to have multiple containers and keep only one size of clothing in each. Labeling (see Systems, below) is the best means of locating what you need, but another useful visual aid is to use a size of container that corresponds to the clothing size: bigger sizes in bigger containers.

- **Simplify** Remember to use what you have. Your hand-me-down storage system is not going to be photographed, so there's no need to have brand-new containers that match. Keep it simple. If anything, see-through can be very useful for easy retrieval.

- **Systems** Keep boxes together, in one place. Create labels that are large enough to read and

CREATING A HOMEWORK STATION

Use your head to make sure your student shines brightly at school. Here are some A+ ideas for creating an ideal study space at home.

File it!
A binder or basic file box, organized by subject, helps manage projects, assignments, tests and study guides.

Bin it!
A trash can and recycling container placed next to the desk will remind students to toss food wrappers and unnecessary papers, so keeping their workspace tidy.

Space
Make sure the desk or work surface is at least 30 in (76 cm) wide—large enough to hold a computer, mouse and books.

Comfort first
An adjustable chair allows the student to be positioned at the correct height for the desk, and padding and a supportive backrest will keep them seated comfortably and working productively.

Light
Situate the desk in natural light, if possible, and add a bright light for evening study sessions.

Protect power
Use a surge protector for cords and cables, including computer, phone charger and printer.

Desk protector
A plastic or plexiglass blotter protects the desk surface and allows students to personalize their space by adding stickers to the top or photos and postcards underneath.

uncomplicated (painter's tape and a big, bold marker will work fine). Make a master list where everything is logged in and out, and keep that in an easy-to-access place (like on a clipboard next to the washer).

■ **Specify** Be descriptive and consistent when labeling containers. You can categorize your size box further by specifying season or type. For example, "2T Summer" and "2T Winter," or "2T Long" for long-sleeved shirts and long pants and "2T Short" for short sleeves and shorts.

PLAYROOM PARADISE
If you have the space for a separate playroom, make sure it doesn't turn into a dumping ground for everything that won't fit in the bedroom. Start by deciding how many big items will be kept in the playroom. Things like a drum set, ping-pong table or pint-sized grocery store can't be "put away." Then use the principles discussed in Storing Toys (page 68) to contain the smaller items.

CONTROLLING SCHOOL-KID CLUTTER
During a child's school career, they will inevitably come home with more "stuff" than they left with. From the get-go, it makes sense to have a strategy that eliminates the accumulation of excess school days clutter.

GENIUS AT WORK
Lunch boxes, tin buckets and cloth bins (above left) hold a plethora of study and creative supplies for a petite powerhouse.

PLATFORM SLEEPING
When no one wants the top bunk, platform beds and a trundle to the rescue (above). Here, sleeping accommodations for three combine with wide, deep drawers that mean clothing, blankets and linens—things that would normally be stored in a traditional chest—take up no extra space. And no more checking under the bed for monsters.

❶ Final exam
Immediately after the school year ends and final grades are received, tackle locker and book-bag clutter. Sort through stuff that isn't going to make the next grade and dismiss it forever.

❷ Textbooks
There are very few reasons to hang on to textbooks. As soon as possible, resell or trade them at academic bookstores or online vendors, or make inquiries about donating them to a prison education program or needy school.

❸ Art projects
There's no reason to store every popsicle-stick picture frame that comes home. At the end of the year, sort through everything that's been kept, and select only a few favorites.

❹ Science experiments
The solar-system diorama that earned a gold star can be photographed and remembered forever, but it doesn't need to sit around eternally.

❺ School supplies
Dried-out markers; scribbled, doodled, coverless notebooks; cracked pens; and stubby pencils can be tossed in the trash.

❻ Keepsakes
Ribbons, medals, trophies, awards, certificates—it seems like everyone's a winner. Hanging on to everything makes nothing special. So let go of the award that everyone on the team received, and keep only the truly special ones.

❼ Shop from home
Children's birthdays generate all sorts of clutter, and it's inevitable that kids will receive duplicate books, games or gifts. Stash the doubles all together in a box then, when it's time for the next party, "shop" first from the comfort of your own closet.

❽ Party favors
Bags filled with cheap, meaningless stuff just add to the clutter conundrum. Teach kids the art of politely refusing it with a "thank you" at the party or discarding the junk once they are home. When it's your turn to host the party, become a trendsetter—implement a minimalism movement by banishing loot bags.

Ages and stages of activity

Babies, toddlers, small children

- **Activities include:** *Sleeping, playing, reading.*
- **Storage for:** *Large plastic and wooden toys, board books, stuffed animals, everyday clothes, costumes.*

The baby's nursery is fun to organize, because everything that needs to be contained is tiny and adorable! There are usually fresh new things that deserve tender loving care, just like a baby.
The best way to start organizing is by working with the biggest piece of furniture, typically a tall dresser or low chest of drawers. In many homes, the chest of drawers doubles as a changing table, which requires a place for both clean and dirty diapers. A crib, rocking chair or bookcase might be included, too. Some pieces of furniture will grow with the child, like a crib that converts into a toddler's bed. A rocking chair can be kept, recushioned and used for many years as the child grows.

UNDERCOVER STORAGE
In a younger child's room, underbed toy storage (bottom left) means that trains, planes and automobiles are easily accessible and easily tucked away later.

SHOE-IN
Over-the-door shoe pockets aren't just for shoes (bottom center). They hold hair accessories, dolls, arts, crafts and much more.

HANG IT UP
If walls wore aprons or pants with deep pockets (bottom right), imagine the goodies they'd contain: books, marbles, markers and miniature figurines—oh my!

Tweens and teens

- **Activities include:** *Sleeping, relaxing, creating, studying.*
- **Storage for:** *Games, books, clothing, uniforms, keepsakes, accessories, sporting and music equipment, toiletries, cosmetics.*

As kids grow up, they tend to accumulate more things. But adding more storage and organization aids isn't the answer. At this point in a child's life, the organizing process needs to be a little more interesting and as uniquely suited to the child's lifestyle as possible. Tweens crave novelty, but constantly coming up with fresh items that suit their rapidly changing preferences can be financially challenging. Therefore, it's wise to invest in storage solutions that can repurposed—for example, wooden furniture that can be repainted or "pimped" with washi tape.

SIMPLE SOLUTIONS
Open units make it so easy to put books, folders and toys away. Baskets are easily pulled out and cuddlies can be thrown in. A blanket box makes great storage for dressing-up clothes; again, they are simply thrown in at the end of the day.

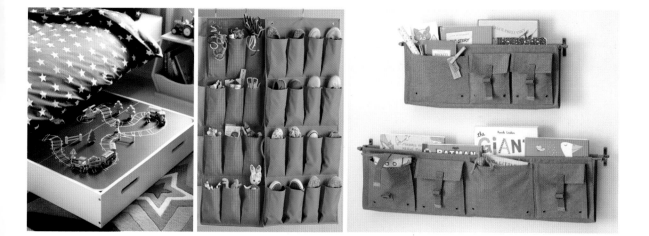

Master bedroom

Where we sleep, clutter creeps. When it comes to organizing, bedrooms are often low on the priority list, and as a result may be the least organized rooms in our homes. Clutter accrues slowly and stays put because bedrooms aren't "public" rooms; they aren't seen by guests, and the clutter can be kept behind closed doors.

It is all too easy to let your bedroom become your dirty little secret, a resting place for stuff that doesn't—as yet—have a permanent home. But your bedroom should be a sanctuary, a tidy, peaceful space where you can relax and rejuvenate without constant reminders of undone chores.

WHY MAKE IT?

The focal point of the master bedroom is, of course, the bed, which makes it the perfect place to begin organizing.

I believe the act of making the bed every morning to be an important one, but there are those that think, why bother, when it's going to get unmade again at the end of the day, and no one is going to see it anyway? Why waste the time and energy? Well, because making the bed starts the day on a positive note and can initiate momentum for crossing other items off the to-do list. There's a sense of "mission accomplished" once the bed is made. Making the bed every morning is not a singular act in itself, but the precursor to a clutter-free day.

The amount of stuff you like to use to dress your bed—pillows, comforters, throws—is a matter of personal preference. But take into account the daily task of making the bed and ask yourself whether all those blankets and throws are worth the extra effort required to replace them every day?

ON YOUR MARKS

When attacking a bedroom that needs a thorough declutter, start with an unmade bed. Strip the bed and toss the mattress pad into the washing machine. Check the care label on the pillows and, if it is safe to do so, pop them in the dryer on high heat for 30 minutes to kill germs and to fluff and freshen them. Rotate the mattress so that the foot portion moves to the head of the bed.

While the mattress pad is washing and drying, gather together four sturdy containers—anything you have available, laundry baskets, perhaps—a few ziplock plastic bags and at least one trash bag. Designate the four large containers as follows:

- **Clothes** For clothes that belong in this room.
- **Donate** Anything that you haven't worn or used in the last six months, or didn't even know you had, can be donated.
- **Keep** Use this container for the nonclothing items that will stay in the room.
- **Relocate** Place in this container all those items that should not even be in this room in the first place!

The ziplock bags are for small pieces that might get lost in one of the larger containers, such as

FORM AND FUNCTION
Making the bed every morning reinforces that tiny tasks matter. A made bed is: good for the soul; flattering to the rest of the bedroom; and an excellent investment of 60 seconds. Piece together store-bought bookshelves for customized easy-access storage for weekend read-a-thons, and display only a few favorite collectibles for a restful retreat.

keys, jewelry, coins and stamps. The trash bag is
for anything that needs trashing.

THE FIRST PUSH

Start by decluttering the floor, beginning at the
door. Work around the room in a clockwise
motion, picking up everything that doesn't
belong there. Throw away trash and put all
other items in their designated containers. Do
not leave the room to return things to their
"homes," since this will be done later.

Once the floor is clear, turn your attention to
each piece of bedroom furniture, removing
items resting on them that don't belong.
Consider each item on the top of the dresser or
nightstand and put back only the necessary

ones. While horizontal surfaces seem to attract
clutter, so do exercise machines, electronics and
pet beds. Continue sorting the items into the
designated containers.

Next, venture under the bed. Pull loose items
out and sort them into the containers. Storage
boxes or bags that you have previously packed
and labeled thoughtfully—perhaps when
decluttering a closet—can be left.

THE BIGGER PICTURE

Consider whether there are any superfluous
pieces of furniture that can be removed from
the room—an unused exercise bike, perhaps, or
an armchair that is never sat on, except by a pile
of laundry. Less furniture means less to clean

SOLO
Do you need more than a place to put your watch, water glass and reading material? If you're going to keep something, give it a place in your home. Enjoy the items you own.

and maintain, and, most importantly, fewer surfaces to become cluttered again.

CLOTHES

Take everything out of the dresser drawers, emptying it all onto the bed. Evaluate each item and don't put back anything that isn't comfortable, relevant, in working condition or doesn't fit—even if you think you might fit into it if you lose a few pounds. As you return items to the drawers, put like with like (see Closets: Organizing Options, page 82).

THE FINISH LINE

Now that a complete room of clutter has been reduced to four containers, a trash bag and a few ziplock bags, the process of organizing what remains is far more approachable.

Return the items in the "Clothes," "Keep" and "Relocate" containers to their proper homes. Refer to the advice given for the other rooms in this book to help you with the "Relocate" container.

Load the "Donate" container straight into the car, and make a note in your diary of when you will take it to the thrift store. Take out the trash.

When the mattress pad is clean and dry, put it back on the bed and make the bed up with clean sheets.

Now at bedtime your decluttered space will ensure you feel calm and relaxed, and the room you wake up to will make you feel wonderful!

HIS AND HERS
Install independently controlled reading spotlights above the head of the bed to eliminate the need for bedside lamps. Drawers at the foot of the bed store off-season blankets; his-and-hers built-ins under the bookshelves hold regularly used clothing.

UNDERBED STORAGE
Underbed storage is a great
opportunity to make more space
in your home. In this interior, the
wheeled storage unit doubles as a
low table, a place to rest a cup
and a reading light.

ADDRESSING THE FURNITURE

Choosing bedroom furniture shouldn't be an emotional decision, but one dictated by the dimensions of the room. If the bedroom furniture is too big, the space will feel crowded and not at all relaxing. Choice of colors, fabrics and textures, on the other hand, can be based on emotion and personal preference.

A typical master bedroom includes a bed, perhaps a headboard, a nightstand or two, an armoire or closet and a dresser. These are your essentials. A bedroom may also feature a bench or daybed, chairs, a television and bookshelves. You need to establish which of these items you actually use and therefore need.

Consider the following typical furniture dimensions in relation to your room size, either when first furnishing the room—if you have that luxury—or when deciding whether you might benefit from less furniture or more.

■ **Master bed and headboard** Queen-size mattresses measures 60 x 80 in. (152 x 203 cm) and king are 76 x 80 in. (193 x 203 cm). Headboards and footboards add an additional 10–20 in. (25–50 cm) head to foot, while a full

frame adds an additional 5–10 in. (12.5–25 cm) on the sides. You will need at least 2 ft (60 cm) all around the sides and foot of the bed for access and comfortably changing sheets.

■ **Dresser and armoire** Almost every master bedroom includes a dresser and/or an armoire. A typical six-drawer rectangular dresser measures 60 x 20 in. (152 x 50 cm) wide and is 30 in. (76 cm) tall. An armoire is typically 60 x 17 in. (152 x 42 cm) and is 60 in. (152 cm) tall. When choosing a dresser and armoire, consider also the depth and be aware that they should have 3 ft (1 m) of space in front for drawers and doors to open fully.

If you have a lot of clothes and personal items and not a lot of space, the armoire adds almost double the height in storage while taking up the same amount of square footage as a dresser. See Closets (pages 82–87) for ideas of how to maximize storage in an armoire.

■ **One nightstand** While it is usual to see nightstands in pairs, there is nothing to say you can't have only one in a room. The items you most want to keep at arm's length from the bed—reading light, book, TV remote control—will determine the optimum size, height and

EMBRACE SPACE
Our possessions narrate the twists, turns and transitions of our lives. Mindfully decluttering is a gentle way to start fresh. Practice living with less. There's no reason to live in the past. Having room to walk around, exercise or pull open drawers is a luxury. There's a joyfulness in decluttering and living with less.

3 Maintain the calm

Now that you have created your calming bedroom space, use the following checklists to make sure it stays that way.

1 Weekly to-dos
- Change the sheets.
- Dust the furniture, including lamps, ceiling fan and TV.
- Vacuum the carpet.

2 Monthly check
Go back to the beginning of this chapter. Survey the space to ascertain whether old habits are creeping in. If they are, take out those four containers (see On Your Marks, page 75) and get clearing.

3 Seasonal maintenance
- Mattress—flip in the fall, spin in the spring.
- Fluff pillows in the dryer.
- Replace pillows in years ending in "5" or "0."
- Dry-clean or machine-wash window treatments, bedspreads, bedskirts and blankets.
- Schedule a carpet cleaning or rent a machine.
- Wash the windows.

HAVE IT YOUR WAY
Once you get rid of the stuff you don't need, you'll figure out exactly what you do need. For some, that means shunning a traditional dresser or chest of drawers and opting for open shelving. For others, a dresser helps them keep items orderly. It's a matter of personal choice.

shape of your nightstand. If you need to keep your cellphone close by at night, try to position the nightstand near an electric socket so that you can recharge it while you sleep. As well as a surface for lighting, a glass of water and bedtime reading, the nightstand can be dual purpose, with many featuring drawers, cupboards or cubby holes for storage of smaller items such as undergarments, hand cream or reading glasses.

■ **Media storage** Not necessarily the focal point of the bedroom, but definitely the focal point from the bed, if your bedroom features a television, media storage needs to include a unit that can physically hold the TV with no fear of it falling over. It has to have ample room for speakers and accessories and a neat way of managing and hiding cords. The height of the TV should be about eye level when you are lying on the bed.

Closets

S chedules and inboxes aren't the only
things overstuffed. Chances are your
bedroom closets are, too. If you open
them to toppling towers of T-shirts and
multiple pairs of black pants and jeans,
then you've come to the right place.

Coordinating the chaos in closets doesn't
have to be complicated—something to keep in
mind when you face the seemingly daunting
task. Organizing isn't a one-size-fits-all job,
however, since no two closets or people are
alike. Hanging everything on matching hangers
and stuffing stockings into cute containers isn't
the solution for a disorganized closet. What you
need to do first is attend to the contents, then
you can have fun with the gizmos that go in it.

GETTING STARTED

Begin by removing everything from the closet,
whether hanging, on shelves or in drawers.
Organize the clothes using your preferred
method of categorizing (see Organizing
Options, below). Now is the perfect time to
weed out what you no longer need (see How
To Let Go, page 84), since it's much easier to let
go of things when everything is right there in
front of you. You may not realize you own a
dozen pashmina wraps until you see them all in
the same place at the same time.

Once you have a clear picture of what needs
to go back into the closet, you can make an
informed decision as to what accessories you
need. Hanging rods and hangers, shelves,
drawers and shoe storage systems may require
consideration, and you will find more advice
with regards to choosing them on these pages.

Before putting anything away, vacuum the
entire closet. Dust mites destroy fabrics and are
horrible for people with allergies.

ORGANIZING OPTIONS

A custom-built closet, crafted with your unique
needs in mind, is a sight to behold, and if you
have the means, then enjoy putting it together,

> **"Great closets
> offer both visibility
> and accessibility."**

using the tips and ideas on these pages to get it right. However, customizing a closet can be costly. Another option is to learn the techniques used by the professionals, so that you can transform your disorganized closet—starting with its contents—and reap the rewards.

Great closets offer visibility and accessibility. People wear what they see and can access easily. Just as our wardrobes change and transition, so should our closets. For this reason, overly planned and permanent closet designs are not always a good fit. Once you have made the initial wardrobe cull and discarded what you no longer wear, you can begin reorganizing your closet as follows.

■ **Color** Many people like to organize their clothing by color. Using this approach, it becomes clear with a glance which colors are favorites and which are not. If you have garments in turquoise, orchid and emerald but none in red, yellow or orange, it's obvious you prefer a cool color palette—useful to know when you next go shopping.

Arranging by color also creates a visually pleasing look in the closet. Some experts will suggest arranging garments in order of ROY G BIV—red, orange, yellow, green, blue, indigo, violet, the colors of the rainbow—while others want heavy, dark garments on the left and lighter colors and fabrics on the right, to give

5 How to let go

Regardless of its size, a well-organized closet is a pleasure to own, but to keep it looking that way you need to keep on top of things. To make the necessary adjustments to maintain order, spend time in the closet at the end of each season to decide if there are any pieces that can be donated, considering the following points:

1 What doesn't belong?
Aim to keep only wearable items in the closet. Get rid of things that don't fit, aren't comfortable or are out of style. Any keepsake garments you no longer wear, like a wedding dress or college T-shirt, should be moved out (see Safely Storing Keepsake Clothes, opposite).

2 Partner pieces
Make sure the items you keep have at least two companion pieces. Remove items that can't be worn with anything else.

3 Bottoms up
If you are stacking T-shirts or jeans, note how long the items at the bottom of the pile have been there, untouched. Items that have been on the bottom for months can go. Items worn frequently will stay toward the top of the pile.

4 Disregard value
When evaluating what's in the closet, try to disregard how much money you spent on an item. If it's no longer being worn, no matter how much it cost to buy, let it go. It's taking up very valuable closet space.

5 What else can go?
Without thinking twice, these other items should be donated to the thrift store:
- Trophy-sized items that used to fit but are too small now.
- Garments rarely worn because they require too much ironing, dry-cleaning or other forms of high maintenance.
- Shoes that can't be worn comfortably to walk a flight of stairs or stand for a few hours.
- Handbags that are ridiculously large, heavy or encourage carrying around more than is necessary.

CLOSET CONFIGURATION
There are several options for configuring a custom-built closet. Before ordering, do some investigation. What widths and depths are available for shelves and drawers? Do you want rails, racks or shelves for shoes, and how many pairs of shoes will fit on each? Can the pieces be reconfigured easily?

1 A light-colored finish keeps clothing colors clear and crisp; no more mixing up blacks and blues.

2 Shelving, strategically placed above hanging rods, allows for even more storage; perfect for hats, luggage and handbags.

3 Double hanging rods make good use of vertical space. Make sure the higher rod is not positioned too high for access.

4 When packing shelves, place the most frequently used items at, or near, eye level.

5 Slippery scarves, silky lingerie and workout wear are difficult hang; they do better in easily accessed drawers.

clothes a visual "lift," as if floating off the rod. Still others will organize by color and type (see below). Dual organizing!

■ **Type** Organizing a closet by type means grouping like with like. Most people do this naturally, positioning tops, bottoms and dresses in separate sections. Some people get even more specific, grouping sleeveless tops, then short sleeves, then long. Still others also color code within their groupings.

One of the perks of organizing by type is that it's easy to spot an abundance or deficit of tops or bottoms, or of particular seasonal garments. One of the disadvantages is that by looking into the closet it may not be immediately obvious to see how outfits can be successfully put

SHOE SIZE
Shoe storage comes in the form of shelves, boxes, pockets, racks and cubbies. Make sure the system you choose is big enough to take the width of the largest shoe size you need to house. Use larger storage for boots.

together. It's worthwhile to spend some time assembling outfits to assess what you have and what you are missing. This can reveal the deficits and the multiples, which can help you avoid buying duplicates on your next shopping trip. Once you've done this, you can create a digital or hard-copy lookbook of photographs of the outfits you have put together, as a useful, quick reference guide.

■ **Capsule** The third way to organize the closet is by capsule, where individual pieces are combined into outfits that offer maximum use. Both high-end and moderate fashion designers create new capsules every season; it's simply a collection of pieces that work together. Everything is coordinated. Top options—sweaters, blouses, shirts, tunics, tanks, jackets and cardigans—all work with bottoms—skirts, shorts and pants. Within those groups, solids hang together, and prints are clustered, too. Each season has a few classics or basics as well as a few trendy items, but the most practical wardrobe should contain as many interchangeable items as possible.

Capsules are adaptable to any lifestyle. A work-from-home woman may create a jean capsule, while a public speaker may create a traditional work capsule. You can also put together separate capsules for outerwear, lingerie, special-occasion clothing and many other possibilities.

The advantage to this system is that it's concise and efficient. If you find you have "lonely" garments not being worn, try organizing by capsules to work those pieces in , or make a list of new items that could be all that is needed to tie it all together.

BUILDING A BETTER CLOSET

There's no shortage of products available to assist in organizing one's belongings. Before investing, take a look at some of the basics that can be purchased *à la carte* from a variety of stores with varying price points. Essentials include a full-length mirror, bright lighting and a variety of hangers (see Hang It Up!, page 87).

SAFELY STORING KEEPSAKE CLOTHES

When you have sorted through your closet, you may well come across clothes that can be stored elsewhere—perhaps in an attic—such as summer clothes in winter, or your wedding dress. Follow this advice for safe storage.

Start by dry-cleaning or washing clothes to be stored, since antiperspirant, makeup residue and cologne will attract insects. Make sure they dry completely to avoid accumulating musty smells and mildew.

Clothes need fresh air, so do not store them in plastic bags. Cotton zip-up bags are a good choice, or buy archival storage containers, which have been treated to preserve and protect fabrics from dust, acid, pests and light—there are even containers specifically designed for wedding dresses. Use acid-free tissue to fill out sleeves and soften any folds, which can cause the fibers in the garment to break down, and wrap the whole item in more acid-free tissue before placing it in the bag. Ensure that the clothes are not stored anywhere that can become damp.

10 Visibility and accessibility

Use these tips to ensure the contents of your closet can be seen and accessed easily.

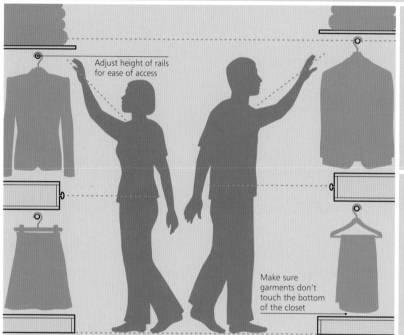

Adjust height of rails for ease of access

Make sure garments don't touch the bottom of the closet

5 Unrestricted hanging
Install hanging rods about 13 in. (33 cm) away from the back wall. This distance allows a little room beyond the ends of the hangers so that clothes won't touch the wall. If you are using extra-large hangers, which are typically 18 in (45.5 cm), the hanging rod will need to be adjusted.

6 Let there be light
Great lighting is a must. Brightening a closet will help sort the blacks from the blues, and reveal any stains, loose threads or missing buttons before you get dressed. While other lighting in the home can be softer, the closet is one area where a light touch isn't the brightest idea. Practicality trumps mood when it comes to lighting a closet.

1 Double hanger
Double your storage space by installing one closet rod approximately 40 in. (100 cm) above the floor and a second one about 40 in. (100 cm) above that. Adjust rods up or down, depending on your height and the height of the closet: You want to reach clothes easily, but you don't want garments touching the floor.

2 High shelves
Shelves let you keep sweaters neatly stacked. If you plan to install shelves above the top hanging rod, make them no deeper than 12 in. (30 cm), so that items can easily be seen and retrieved.

3 Freedom of movement
Rub hanging rods with wax paper to help the hangers glide smoothly along the rod.

4 Low shelves
If you plan to install shelves below eye level (more usual in a walk-in closet as opposed to a reach-in closet), the shelves should be no more than 16 in. (40 cm) deep for easy access.

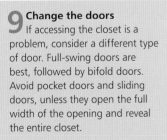

7 Drop in
Pull-out canvas laundry hampers are specialty items, but can be a good addition. Customize your closet to meet your own needs.

8 The choice is clear
Garment bags, shoulder covers, bins and boxes in clear and near-clear vinyl and plastic unify and upgrade a DIY closet.

HANG IT UP

Discard the freebie hangers from the dry-cleaner, and treat your clothes to hangers that will keep them looking their best.

9 Change the doors
If accessing the closet is a problem, consider a different type of door. Full-swing doors are best, followed by bifold doors. Avoid pocket doors and sliding doors, unless they open the full width of the opening and reveal the entire closet.

10 Little extras
Boutique-like acrylic drawers are sized just right for minimalists and of course provide the best visibility.

Wooden, plastic, padded or flocked hangers maintain the shape of a garment best. Shop for hangers that have elongated hooks and contoured shoulders. Long hooks help keep collars in shape, while the shoulders mirror human shoulders and carry the weight of the garment.

Clip and clamp hangers, used for skirts and pants, should have cushioning fabric such as felt or foam to protect crushable fabrics such as corduroy or velour. Open-ended hangers require padding as well, to prevent a knee-level fold in pants.

Bathroom

Bathrooms are unique in that they are both private and public. We take for granted that, once we close the door, the bathroom is "off-limits" to anyone else. However, home bathrooms are public in the sense that everyone in the home, including guests, has access to them.

DAY TO DAY

While bathroom activities are basic and primal, the products in them are quite modern and evolved. Some are used frequently (dental, hair, skin and nail care items) and others only as needed (first-aid products, medications and cleaning supplies). While the "daily stuff" needs to be conveniently located, most of the other stuff can be tucked away in a linen closet or utility area.

Life's little "necessities and niceties" tend to clutter what is the most no-nonsense room in the home. Don't be fooled: The zen-zone bathrooms seen on television and in magazines likely look very different at the end of the day after a family has cycloned through.

Healthy organizing habits are no different than good hygiene habits. Just as regular teeth brushing and flossing require self-discipline learned and practiced daily, the same is needed when the entire family commits to good organizing habits. You can achieve a spa-like environment in the bathroom by keeping clutter to a minimum.

CHOSEN FOR FUNCTION
Pretty décor is pleasing and luxurious amenities are lovely, but bathrooms need easy-to-access storage. In an open shelf unit (right), use open boxes to separate the necessary trappings so they are easy to find and put away. Keep first-aid supplies in a lidded box, but keep the medicines out of reach of very young children. Individual hooks for hand towels and bath towels (left top) keep the floor and the shower rod clutter free. Install a shelf above the hooks for quick access to items used routinely. One unit—both functional and stylish—for soap, lotion and a fingertip towel (left bottom) keeps guest bath countertops clutter free.

NO BATHROOM COUNTERTOP? NO PROBLEM
Let loose your imagination and creativity. Two bath buckets (above) hold products for teens, while a third holds fresh towels. Hooks, to the right of the sink, can be used to hang wet towels.

VINTAGE CHIC
A repurposed glass-front cabinet (above right) works beautifully to provide extra storage for lotions and potions.

LET IT GO

With our stressful lives, it's important, today more than ever, to create a calm, peaceful place to enjoy a few minutes of privacy. It is, after all, called a restroom!

Everyone in the family must agree to bring in only what's necessary. Let go of "someday syndrome"—"Someday I'll use those cosmetic samples," or "Someday I'll clean under the sink and throw away half-empty bottles of hair conditioner and body lotion." Rid the room of:

- Expired sunscreens, vitamins and medications.
- Unused rusty nail clippers and bobby pins, and duplicate lip-pencil sharpeners.
- Free-with-purchase cosmetic bags and unflattering foundations.
- Outdated ointments, lotions and creams.

TYPE AND FREQUENCY

Group the items that are left like with like—medicines, makeup, haircare, dental care—and by frequency of use. Shampoos and shower gels in daily use need to be accessible from the shower. Hairbrushes and styling products, facial moisturizers, shaving foams and makeup should be within easy reach of a mirror, perhaps in a drawer or on shelves under the sink, or in a freestanding organizer positioned next to the sink. Products that are not used every day (first-aid kit, sunscreens, extra supplies of toilet rolls, cleaning products) should be assigned a permanent home in a cupboard, in drawers or boxes, or separate from the bathroom if there is no room left.

7 Tips for giving everything a home

Several family members share the bathroom, making it one of the most heavily frequented rooms of the house. Items need to be accessed and put away easily and quickly.

3 Pull-out shelving
Pull-out shelves, usually found in the kitchen section at home-improvement stores, allow easy access to things kept under the sink or in deep cabinets.

4 Stacking towers of drawers
These can hold a variety of items that need not take up valuable real estate in bigger drawers, such as feminine hygiene supplies, occasionally used ointments, or extra toothbrushes for guests.

6 Baby bathtime
Bathtime for toddlers involves lots of adorable little toys; a mesh bag hung from the wall allows them to dry between bubble baths and keeps the tub and shower clutter-free.

1 Drawer organizers
Organizers in bathroom drawers allow you to keep items separate and easily accessible. Clear acrylic dividers store bobby pins and safety pins together but separately. Makeup and brushes live side by side.

7 Look up
When counter space is limited, think vertically. To ensure the counter isn't strewn with dozens of individual items, use two drawers, one for items used in the morning, the other for items used before bed.

2 Spring-loaded drawer dividers
These are another great option that allows you to divide and conquer the drawer contents. You can arrange them back-to-front or side-to-side.

5 Improvise
Plastic is fantastic for bathrooms without lower cabinets. Stackable, open or see-through containers keep items clean, fresh and dry.

Home office

Anyone working from home knows that having a dedicated space where they can make conference calls, schedule to-dos and pay bills is helpful—even if the "office" moonlights as a guest bedroom or is tucked under a staircase.

BOOSTING PRODUCTIVITY

When it comes to creating a home office, it's all about mixing conventional and unconventional ideas. It seems that everyone is juggling chaotic schedules. In addition, between checking voicemail, email, social media and newsfeeds, we may not be as focused on productivity as we need to be, which means we aren't as organized as we'd like to be. Multitasking isn't always a good idea, even when working from the comfort of home; it often leads to feeling overwhelmed and disorganized. But one of the perks of having a home office is that we can return calls while the laundry is tumbling dry. We can listen to voicemail while walking the dog. And we can file papers while dinner simmers in the crockpot. It's important to note that being productive is different from being organized. Plenty of people who are organized aren't productive. They can find things they need, but they don't cross much off their to-do lists.

Productivity and organization require discipline. By arming yourself with information, education and motivation, you can create a home office you'll enjoy working in and that will increase your productivity.

LESS IS MORE: CATEGORIES FOR HOME FILING

Generally speaking, there are rules that apply to almost any organizing task—for example, keeping like objects together. But there are also techniques for addressing specific challenges, and sometimes the perfect solution is actually a combination of solutions. Personal (not business) filing is an example.

Creating a home filing system involves numerous decisions. Many paper hoarders are paralyzed by perfectionistic tendencies; they'd rather take no action than file something incorrectly or throw away the wrong receipt. Instead, they retain every receipt and slip of paper, likely leaving it on a flat surface somewhere—the top of the fridge, the entryway table, the kitchen countertop or the dresser. Unnecessary receipts are stashed everywhere, yet when needed, the correct receipt simply can't be located.

To begin making sense of all that paperwork, start by sorting papers into the broadest, most basic categories. Broader categories mean fewer files and fewer search possibilities when looking for documents.

The key to creating a successful filing system is to make it as uncomplicated as possible. Three nonconventional but logical categories I use are: Fun, Family and Fact.

■ **Fun** The Fun files contain information about vacation planning, home decorating ideas, sentimental cards and letters, upcoming recreational classes being offered locally, and so on. I suggest picking a color for this file

> 66 The key to creating a successful filing system is to make it as uncomplicated as possible. 99

CONSIDER YOUR OPTIONS
You might choose to store important paperwork vertically in binders, and print and store digital images in archival boxes. Wicker waste baskets hold extra cords and cables, and a stack of shallow drawers sitting under the tabletop can be used for filing or storing office provisions.

BILL SORTING
A small desk holds two magazine boxes for bills; one box is labeled B-15, for bills due before the 15th of the month, and the other A-15 for bills due after the 15th. A fabric and ribbon tufted board displays reminders.

FILE FOR ALL
Tall bookcases serve up plenty of storage in a home office. Window shades reveal and conceal color-coded binders containing marketing, finance and administrative documents. There is no one-size-fits-all solution for filing. Options include magazine holders, binders and various boxes.

(see Color Coding, opposite) that signifies fun and happy, such as yellow (sunshine).

■ **Family** In the Family category are reference files, anything to do with home or family members such as medical records, educational documentation, pets, kids and home maintenance. I suggest picking a color that signifies family, such as red (love).

■ **Fact** The Fact file contains information that needs to be saved as proof if an event of significance were to happen. Anything related to legal or financial matters, taxes insurance property sales and purchases, and receipts for big-ticket items is stored here. Suggested colors are green (money) or blue (trust).

THE PRACTICALITIES OF FILING

Once you have chosen your broad categories, you have a number of options with regards to what you file them into.

■ **Containers** First, decide whether to use file folders, binders or a combination of the two.

There are, of course, more ways to file, but for most people these three options work best. Assess available storage space: if there's room on bookshelves, binders work best; if you are using filing cabinets or filing crates or boxes, file folders work. Consider necessary accessories, too. For example, if you are using binders, you will probably also need page protectors, tab inserts and a hole puncher.

■ **More decisions** File folder options include standard file folders, hanging folders or hanging folders combined with interior standard folders. Select which size file tabs you prefer, one-half, one-third or one-fifth cut tabs: one-third is my preference, and I find one-fifth too small to write on. If using ready-made labels, make sure they fit the cut tabs you prefer before you purchase the file folders.

■ **Labeling** To suit your custom filing needs, DIY labels are best, since you create titles according to your own categories, using a fine-point marker to hand-write them. When selecting hanging file folders, consider those

with built-in tabs. This allows for subcategories. You'll have a general category label on the hanging folder, and subcategories on the labels of the individual files inside.

▪ **Color coding** Color can be used as a device to make retrieval easier. If you decide to use colored folders, start with only three colors (see Less is More: Categories for Home Filing, page 92), and as you build your system, use no more than five.

ACTION FILES

Among the most common organizing challenges homeowners face is dealing with the daily mail and paperwork that requires an action, such as sign and post back, return this portion with your payment, RSVP before a specific date, etc. Some papers need immediate attention, while others can be put aside and dealt with later. Or it may be that we need a reminder later—for example, to mail birthday cards or know when a gift certificate will expire. These are known as action files.

Action files include: Pay, Do, Send, Keep and Read (note, these are all verbs). Some people opt for a Pending file for temporarily keeping event fliers, travel information, meeting information, tickets to events, call-back notes, maintenance reminders and a note of when something will expire.

It's wise to keep action files conveniently located and incorporate them into a system that can be accessed daily, especially after opening the mail or printing something from the computer. While you may be used to placing an invitation under a magnet on the

BOXES AND BINDERS
Book shelves can be kept neat and uncluttered by utilizing baskets, binders and boxes for paperwork and files. Containers from stationery stores are available in a great range of color variations, so you can easily code your storage systems.

fridge, pinning a travel itinerary to a corkboard or leaving a "return with payment" note on the kitchen counter, anything that requires action but is left homeless is a formula for forgetting about it. This is where having a real system works wonders.

The system for action files is a tickler system, also known as the 43 folders system (one folder for each month [12], and one folder for each day of the month [31]). Documents and reminder notes are dropped into the file in the appropriate month and the specific due date— when they need to be dealt with, discussed or contemplated further. The file is checked daily and "tickles" (reminds) you to take action. Folders must be checked daily. If you are a dedicated smartphone user, you can add a secondary tickler system by setting up a daily reminder on your phone's calendar to check that day's tickler file at home.

The tickler system allows you to give items a temporary home and forget about them until you are reminded. This system "tickles" you into remembering what you need to do when.

The system is most effective for temporarily holding papers that represent tasks, but is also effective for holding mental "notes," which you write on paper. You don't want to forget to do something, so you write yourself a note and file it in the date at which you need to be reminded.

The tickler file is like the departure gate at the airport; everyone checks in and waits to board and eventually take off. The tickler file is not the final destination; it holds things and thoughts temporarily. Without the departure gate, passengers would meander and end up who-knows-where when it's time to take off. Without a tickler file your documents and notes would migrate all over the home.

DESKED FOR SUCCESS

If the role of your office space is primarily to deal with the comings and goings of the household, a desk for the computer and a comfy chair are useful, but if you don't have the space you might find yourself using the dining-room table or breakfast bar. Alternatively, a filing system and perfunctory desk might fit in a part of the living room, or be built in to fit under the stairs. If you also work from home,

DIVIDE AND CONQUER!
When families share office spaces, give everyone their own shelf, cubby or cabinet to stay organized in their own unique way. With these bright containers from The Container Store, you can even color code for each family member.

you will want to give the office space further consideration based on the job you do. In the spirit of decluttering and staying organized and productive, don't get carried away buying equipment and accessories that aren't required. You won't necessarily need everything detailed below in your own home-office space, so only choose what you will actually use.

- Comfortable chair and desk
- Footrest under desk
- Filing cabinet and binders
- Computer with monitor and keyboard and/or laptop
- Lighting; natural and lamps
- Mic and camera for video-conferencing
- Phone(s), with a wireless option
- Printer, ink, toner
- Scanner /copier (fax, if needed)
- Shredder
- Surge protectors
- Office supplies—paper, pens, staples, paperclips, scissors, rubber bands, etc

7 Tips for a lean, serene home office

A well-appointed home office is possible with smart solutions to help manage papers, books, cords and more.

4 Portability
Files or folders contained in a desktop box are portable, which means you don't have to keep your files in a dedicated home office, but anywhere that is accessed every day but where they won't get in your way.

5 Consider the light
Natural light and task lighting need thought from both decorative and functional perspectives. Exposure to sunlight boosts mood, so if you can place your desk facing a window you will benefit. Task lighting in the form of a spot desk lamp can be useful, and if you are video-conferencing make sure the light is in front of you.

6 Aim high
When surface space is limited, use the walls. Here, wooden boxes with separate compartments hold office supplies. The boxes can be painted, papered or left natural.

7 Tangled up in tech
To tame the tangle of tech wires, use a cord management kit, clamps, or clips, tape and wraps to attach them to the desk or keep them neatly tied together.

1 Creative filing
Your choice of filing container (whether for home filing or action files) need not be restricted to the advice given here (see The Practicalities of Filing, page 94). You can adapt the techniques described to fit other storage systems, such as clipboards mounted on the wall, recycled extra-large envelopes, labeled baskets or cubbies and sorters.

2 Top up office supplies
Try to keep well stocked with extra office supplies, since printer out-of-ink-emergencies are disruptive to productivity. You could use your tickler file (see page 95) to file regular reminders to order more supplies.

3 Easily found
Wall-mounted bar systems use S hooks to keep favorite office supplies visible and within easy reach.

Storage spaces

For many people, not knowing where to store something translates into "park it in the garage to deal with it later." So the garage is treated as a dumping ground for sporting equipment, Christmas decorations, garden tools and random household objects, with the attic or basement usually serving a similar purpose.

Every home makes use of a space of temporary storage, for the things that we still use, but not often. We need dedicated spaces to store the things we don't really need access to every day, but would rather not get rid of. And there is nothing wrong with that. By decluttering we do not intend to purge everything, but rather minimize what we have and make it easy to find it when we need it. So in the attic you might keep the children's clothes that will be passed on to baby in a few years' time (see Kids Spaces: The 4 S's of Storing Clothes, page 69) and your wedding dress (see Closets: Safely Storing Keepsake Clothes, page 85), which you don't intend to wear again, but of course means a lot to you so cannot be given away. But we do need to be vigilant about what we keep, and instigate an organized means of storage, to ensure these spaces don't become dumping grounds—out of sight out of mind.

ALL HANDS ON DECK
The garage, attic and basement deserves the same treatment as the rest of the home when it comes to decluttering and organizing. They should not serve as a homeless shelter for wayward objects with no permanent residence.

Many of these spaces are not climate controlled, and their rough, unfinished interiors make them less comfortable, less show-worthy spaces to organize than other rooms. This means homeowners are even less enthusiastic about sorting them out.

ALL FOR ONE AND ONE FOR ALL
The garage typically becomes a drop zone for house overflow. It's easy to put stuff out there, delay making decisions and watch it accumulate. Organizing a garage provides an opportunity for the whole family to work together toward a common goal. When everyone collaborates, organizing the largest "room" in the home is fun and productive.

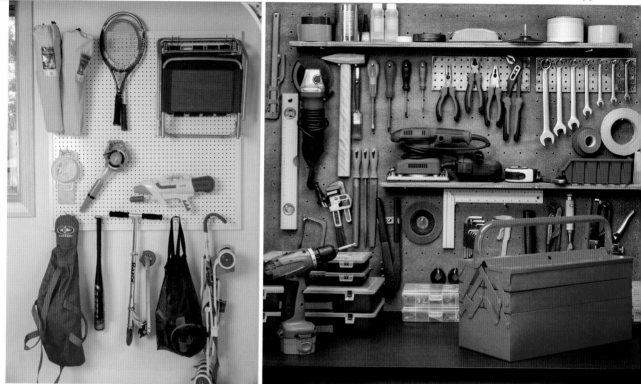

> **When it comes to organization, the garage deserves the same treatment as the rest of the house.**

WALL SYSTEMS
Because pegboard (above) is one of the most versatile, affordable options available, and offers excellent visibility of all items, it's become the go-to tool for organizing storage spaces. Conveniently located tools (above right) are used more often. Simple storage solutions that your grandparents used have become classic methods to make it easier to use what we already have on hand.

The idea of sorting through everything in any of these spaces might well frighten the life out of you, but before you can address "how" you are going to store stuff, you need to make an inventory of "what" you need to store. Then you can more easily decide what style of container or storage system you might need. You can save yourself time and energy by decluttering and sorting these areas now, before things get even more out of hand.

Begin by scheduling a time for decluttering that everyone can commit to. The work will go faster if the entire family, including kids, gets in on the action. Explain that everything needs to be removed from the garage (and yes, that means every single thing!) and divided into specific "departments," just like big-box stores do it. Younger members of the family can use sidewalk chalk to create zones that indicate where things will go once they are pulled out of the garage. Areas might include:

- Trash
- Donate
- Recycle
- Garage sale
- Fix it
- Finish it
- Keep

THE SPORT OF THE SORT

If sorting were a competitive sport, would you take home gold, silver or bronze? You can go for the gold by preparing. Make sure you have the supplies you need on hand to make the process more deliberate and doable: for example, you might want a table for placing objects temporarily, a tarp to place things that shouldn't be put on the ground but are too big for the table, and containers for trash. And don't forget the accessories, such as a wide-tip marker for labeling containers and sidewalk chalk.

Get rid of as much as possible when emptying the storage spaces. In the garage, current lifestyle and available leisure time should be evaluated when determining what to keep and what to let go of. As an example, a family with four pre-teen kids all participating in weekend sports might decide that gardening time is limited, and the gardening workbench might be better used as a science project area. Each garage is unique to the people that use it. Some require multiple zones (see Garage Departmentalizing, page 102), while others just want to park their cars and lawnmower out of the elements.

Perhaps you have been storing items to pass on to your children or grandchildren. Now is the time to ask them if they actually want them, and if so, ask them to take them now. If they don't want them, then you have been given permission to donate them or, if they might be worth something, sell them.

WHAT DO I NEED IN THE GARAGE?

Knowing what to keep and what you can let go of can be problematic, since tools and gardening apparatus are not used every day, and you might be unsure of what you might need in the future.

Years ago, I asked my trusted hired handyman for advice on building a toolkit of my own. A man of few words, he replied, "If it moves and shouldn't, use duct tape. If it doesn't move and should, use WD-40." And it's true—at the most basic level, that's all you need. However, if you think the tasks you take on in the home and garden may require a few extras, decide whether you need the following tools based on the jobs they do.

- **Basic home toolkit** As well as duct tape and WD-40, these tools are used for a variety of tasks and are good to have in a basic kit: hammer (not too heavy, not too light), with nonslip grip handle; flathead (single blade) and Phillips (square) screwdrivers—small and large of each—or one with interchangeable tips; a locking utility knife; a putty knife; a straight-edge metal measuring tape with a soft-grip case and locking button; and a steel square.
- **Cordless drill** A keyless chuck, 12-volt model will get the average homeowner through almost any job. Make sure its grip is rubber-coated and comfortable.
- **Level** Both the pocket and torpedo levels are small enough to fit in tiny spaces, while a carpenter's level is larger. The bubbles inside

indicate when something is perfectly straight. The torpedo level, which checks three planes, is the most useful.

- **Pliers** Traditional slip-joint pliers are useful for loosening nuts and bolts and tightening without stripping. Needle-nose pliers are great for twisting and tightening picture-hanging wire and working in small spaces.
- **Wrench** A must-have for anyone who has ever assembled furniture or removed tight or rusty nuts and bolts. The adjustable wrench adapts for most jobs.
- **Gloves** All-purpose, impermeable work gloves are imperative for keeping hands splinter-, paint- and oil-free.
- **Hardware** Include a supply of anchors, hooks, wood and drywall nails, picture-hanging wire and nails, and wood and metal screws.
- **Painter's tape** Used on a variety of surfaces, it lifts off easily and leaves no residue, even when exposed to heat and sunlight. Use it to mask areas of a wall or woodwork that you don't want to paint, or on walls before hanging art to eyeball arrangements.
- **Velcro and tie wraps** Useful for securing Christmas garlands to railings, keeping computer cords together, temporarily "locking" a suitcase, and a variety of other tasks.

- **Basic garden toolkit** Watering can; trowel; utility bucket; kneeling bench or cushion; and gloves (cotton for light yard work; leather for tough jobs like working with roses and clearing branches and brush; and synthetic, which are thin, flexible and puncture resistant for spreading compost and planting seeds).
- **Planting** A bulb planter lifts plugs of soil for planting bulbs; a dibber pokes holes in soil for seed planting; a cultivator breaks up soil before weeding; and a hand hoe also breaks up the soil and makes trenches.
- **Cutting** A hand pruner to cut branches, rose bushes and large flowers; shears to cut grasses and perennials; scissors to cut herbs, twine and roots and for deadheading; and hedge shears.
- **Weeding** A hand rake to weed between plants, and a weeder for working between pavers and in cracks.

GARAGE FURNITURE

When you know what needs to be kept and accessed in the garage, you can figure out which storage solutions most suit your needs. Options include a workbench, shelves and bins, storage wall systems and overhead storage. Remember, however, that items should be visible and accessible.

ALL ABOUT THAT BASE
The workbench is typically the base of any workstation. Careful consideration should be given to depth, height, lighting and organization of tools used most often.

TO EACH HIS OWN
The contents of a garage and how best to keep them accessible is more about your family's interests and routines than it is any particular method of organizing. Overhead storage and bike racks may be right for a young family, while a keen mechanic or carpenter will have other requirements.

■ **Workbench** Car maintenance, gardening and small DIY repairs require a flat work surface with room to spread out, perhaps accompanied by a vertical system (see page 99), with maybe a pegboard or slat wall, to keep small tools within arm's reach.

■ **Shelves and bins** Labeled plastic bins stacked neatly on shelves, easily pulled out when needed, are ideal for seasonal decorations, camping equipment and home-maintenance items, such as lightbulbs and spare batteries. Bins range in size from shoe box to 120-gallon tubs. Clear containers reveal the contents and can be color coded using duct tape or labels to identify seasonal items or family members' individual bins.

■ **Storage wall system** The options are limited only by budget when it comes to climbing the walls with storage solutions in the garage. A pegboard with hooks holds pliers, hammers and gardening tools. You can use wall panel systems with larger hooks to secure leaf blowers, and cabinets with locks for toxic and flammable products.

■ **Overhead storage** Suspended from the rafters or ceiling, storage racks hold the heaviest of objects, such as bicycles and wheelbarrows and patio furniture, and can be raised and lowered. Smaller, stationary versions keep seasonal items like window screens and coolers handy.

GARAGE DEPARTMENTALIZING

As you return items to the garage, create zones within the space. Categories might include:

■ **Sporting** Sort by person and by season. Fall footballs and shoulder pads in one section; spring golf clubs, soccer balls and skipping ropes elsewhere. Bikes, helmets and skate boards remain out year round in milder climates. Balls could be kept in mesh bags hung from hooks, or in wire baskets on the wall. Stand long items, such as rackets, hockey sticks and golf umbrellas, upright in a trash can or unused golf bag. For bikes, skis, surfboards, long boards and sleds, wall-mounted racks may well be the answer. Hanging tote bags and portable canvas bins are good for grab-and-go outings, such as a pool tote, which would include a frisbee, swim goggles, sunscreen and beach balls.

■ **Holiday** Sort vacation items like with like and by season, so you can grab what you need when you need it. Use color-coded labels

8 Tips for a successful garage sale

One man's trash is another man's treasure, and what better way to prove this than with a garage sale. Items in the "Donate" and "Recycle" piles of your garage clearout can be offered for sale to neighbors, friends and passersby, along with anything you have cleverly gleaned from other rooms in the home. Follow these tips to make sure the sale is stress-free and a huge success.

1 Choose a date wisely
You can increase your chances of attracting buyers by cleverly choosing when to hold your sale. April, May, June and September are good months for garage sales, and since the 1st or the 15th day of the month is payday for many, it makes sense to hold your sale near one of these dates. Saturdays and Sundays are a sensible choice, and early in the day is better than later.

2 Spread the word
Start by letting neighbors know about your sale, both as potential customers and in case they have any concerns. For example, if they don't want strangers parking in front of their homes, place "no parking" signs where appropriate. You could place an advertisement in a local newspaper, or post signs in the neighborhood, on a nearby community board or at the grocery store. Contact local authorities to inquire about restrictions, permits regulations, etc. for posting signs and hosting sales.

3 Setup
Make the sale stress-free with preparation. Make sure that items are in reasonable condition or better. Organize items like with like. Some categories are: clothing (men, women, children, babies), toys, books, appliances, dishes and kitchen items, decorative items, furniture, and sports gear. You will need display tables and an assortment of bags—a good opportunity to recycle plastic or paper grocery bags or gift bags. Additional extras might include:

- Bubble wrap and newspapers for fragile items or breakables.
- Tape to secure lids or keep stray pieces together.
- Permanent markers to change price signs throughout the day.
- Calculators for adding up sales.
- Extension cords to show that electrical items work.
- Spare lightbulbs if selling lamps.
- Batteries for testing toys and small appliances.

4 Bargain to sell
People come to a garage sale looking for a good deal, so don't get offended if customers try to "bargain down." Remember that your motive is to declutter; making money is secondary.

5 Leftovers
Do NOT bring the items that didn't sell back into your home or garage. Instead, and immediately after the sale, either:

- Drive them to the nearest donation center.
- Place them curbside with a sign that says, "FREE—Help Yourself!" Trash anything that remains after two days.

6 Price it right
Rather than pricing every single item for sale, group similar items together on a table and price them all the same. To make mental arithmetic less challenging, price in 50-cent increments.

7 Money matters
Have a cash-only rule, and get some small bills and change, for change, from the bank before the sale. Take collected money inside your house periodically.

8 Advertise clearly
Don't forget the obvious and make sure your advertising features the date, time and address. You may want to list a rain date, or have an indoor backup plan. Be creative with your wording and maybe list a few "big ticket" items to draw interest.

on boxes to make the one you need easy to spot from a distance—especially helpful when storing in overhead racks.

■ **Tools** Hardware stores have this figured out, so don't reinvent the wheel. First, sort by broad category: plumbing, electrical, painting, construction. Then sort hardware and small tools by task: cutting, drilling, nailing, gluing.

■ **Car care** If you are a keen mechanic and have a large collection of car care equipment, sort and segregate it all by function, such as washing, maintenance and repair.

■ **Recreation** Sort by season for ease of access. Summer days spent at the beach or soccer field may require access to coolers, sun umbrella and lawn chairs, while winter activities might require snowboards, skis, sleds and skates.

■ **Yard, lawn, gardening** Begin by sorting by task, including planting, watering, fertilizing, mowing, trimming and snow blowing. Store fuel tanks for gas-powered tools safely. Further sorting, by size, may also be necessary. Tools with long handles are hazardous when left leaning on walls, so store them in racks with clips or slide-in tube-type containers.

OTHER STORAGE REQUIREMENTS

Packaging from electronics or small appliances is often kept in the garage, attic or basement. Since it's almost impossible to put small appliances back in their original Styrofoam packing blocks, only keep the boxes, and discard the cushioning pieces. Keep the boxes only of items that are more of an investment and worth repairing, such as those for the computer, printer or stereo. Ditch the boxes from items you'd most likely replace instead of repair or return.

Storing photos in the basement or attic is not advised, due to the extremes in temperature. Other keepsake items should be carefully packaged, preferably in plastic boxes (see I Can See Clearly Now, right).

HAZARDOUS MATERIALS STORAGE

Toxic cleaners, antifreeze and flammable pesticides and paint thinners are dangerous to children and pets and must be kept out of reach in a locked metal or heavy-duty plastic cabinet situated "off the beaten path" and clearly marked "Hazardous" or "Dangerous" so

anyone—including emergency workers in the case of a fire—know that it could be explosive. Do not keep flammable substances, such as gasoline, propane, turpentine or oil-based paints, near any heat sources, including heating systems, water heaters and portable heaters.

FOOD AND BEVERAGE STORAGE

On the "family friendly" side of the basement, located as far away from hazardous material as possible, you can create an overflow pantry storage area. Store surplus food, beverages and cooking supplies on sturdy shelves or palettes raised off the floor with blocks or bricks. Put heavier items on the bottom shelves and lighter items, like paper products, on the top shelves. Newest items should be put at the back of the shelves so older items are used first. Make sure bottles of wine and canned drinks aren't stored near hot-water pipes, boilers or dryer vents.

I CAN SEE CLEARLY NOW

Cloth, wood, wicker and cardboard storage containers do not hold up in basements and attics, since over time they deteriorate and attract bugs. Because attics can become very hot, glass, metal, ceramic and some plastics will fare better than anything with glue, wax and porous or biodegradable components.

The best solution is thick, clear plastic bins with color-coded hinged lids: blue for Hanukkah, red for Christmas, black for Halloween, etc. The transparent bins let you see what's inside and how much of it without having to open it. Plus, they stack on top of each other when the lid is closed and nest inside, whether open or closed. Another perk is that these hinged bins can be locked using a tie-wrap or a padlock secured through the holes on each side.

Alternatively, any box made from thick plastic can be used. It's a good idea, even when using transparent containers, to add two large labels to each container, one on top, another on the side, identifying what's inside.

Store the heaviest boxes on the bottom of the stack to avoid cracking the lids. For stacks of multiple units, consider investing in a steel paneled dolly on rolling casters, especially if the entire stack needs to be moved often.

8 Get the best use out of your basement and attic

Declutter and organize your basement or attic so that it will work hard for you. Use these tips to maintain that order and usefulness.

3 In the trusses
Utilizing the small spaces between attic trusses will add a lot of extra storage space. To avoid stacking containers on top one another, install affordable shelving between beams. Having small shelves allows the containers to slide out like drawers.

5 Pest free
To remove musty odors, purchase activated charcoal, and avoid using coffee beans in paper bags which will only attract rodents and bugs. Do not store bags of pet food in the basement as they, too, attract pests.

4 Basement or attic?
Things stored in the basement are generally easier to access, so this can be a good place to store canned and bottled items purchased in bulk. However, the basement may be prone to flooding and dampness, meaning it is not ideal for storing upholstered furniture, clothing, books or documents. The warmer, drier attic would be better suited to these items.

6 Elevate
Use bricks or cinder blocks to elevate pallets or boxes off the basement floor.

1 Size matters
Small and medium-size bins, like these from The Container Store, are easier to manage than one large bin. Depending on the weight of what's being stored, larger bins can be heavy and awkward to tote up and down steps or remove when stacked. Plus, larger containers hold more stuff, which means searching through them may be a drawn-out process of emptying the contents on the floor and putting everything back in again.

2 Bright and inviting
Provide the brightest lighting you can. Paint the basement walls and window ledges bright white to reflect light. Hang mirrors, if possible, to help bounce light around dark areas.

7 Hot and cold
Address safety issues in your attic before making it a storage area. Even though it is dry, an attic is exposed to temperature extremes, very hot in summer and very cold in winter. Not everything will do well stored in such an area. For safety, ensure that your attic, especially in an older house, has a fan or adequate venting.

8 Paint tips
When storing paint, in the garage or basement only, dip the end of a wooden paint stick in each color, and on the other end of the paint stick, note the brand, color name and number, and rooms where it was used. Keep the colored paint sticks with paint supplies or decorating files. Example: Sherwin Williams 6402; Sea Salt; eggshell; mudroom.

Linen closet

Perhaps you've seen the trance-inducing videos where the camera zooms in on a pair of hands as they fold fitted bed sheets into origami-like rectangles of precise perfection. By the time those nimble hands are gently tucking the flat and fitted sheets into crisp, smooth cases, you've convinced yourself that you, too, will take time to master this task and do it every week after laundering towels and sheets. But reality sets in, and you realize it's much easier to wash, dry, and never fold sheets again; just grab them from the dryer, put them back on the beds and avoid the Zen-folding practice.

Organizing your linen closet is not about precision folding or stacking perfectly arranged linens. It is about tackling the problem now, before things get worse. Begin by pulling everything out and grouping items into piles of like with like. Warning: it gets messy, since the average disorganized linen closet may harbor a jumble of items including: bedding (pillows, sheets, blankets, quilts, throws); bathroom accessories (washcloths, bath mats, hand, body and beach towels); dining accessories (tablecloths, place mats, napkins); health and beauty products (vitamins, lotions, medications, first-aid supplies); maintenance items (lightbulbs, batteries, tools); and cleaning tools and materials (task-towels, disinfectants, cleaners, oils, waxes, polishes).

UTILITY TOWELS

Start by separating the utility towels from those that are being used by family members after showering. Use a permanent laundry marker, and in large letters label the utility towels according to their use. For example, on towels used to clean and polish wood floors, write "FLOOR—WASH" and/or "FLOOR—WAX." Other category suggestions include: pets; glass and mirrors; tubs and sinks; toilets; countertops; and fridge and oven.

Alternatively, write the type of product that will be used on the cloth, such as floor wax, glass cleaner or disinfectant, to avoid cross-

COLOR CALMS THE CHAOS
Color coding helps keep family members' blankets, sheets and towels easily identified. Keeping everything in order is particularly important when the contents of your linen closet are on show.

contamination. If you've ever attempted to clean a mirror with a task-towel that had been used to wax furniture, you know it gets very messy very quickly, even after the towels have been laundered, since oil and wax leave a residue.

There's no need to keep too many utility towels, because they last a long time and are easily obtained.

TWO'S COMPANY

Most homes have an abundance of sheets and towels—to put it mildly, more than they need, use, or have space for. Keep just enough bedding and towels so your home functions for a week (or two, at the very most) without laundering. This usually means two sets of sheets per bed (unless there's a need for more—for example, if you have young children or frequent houseguests) and two towels per person: one set will be in use, and one will be waiting in the closet.

If, after sorting, you have items left over, animal shelters appreciate bath and bedding donations; check locally for specifics and donate what you can.

If you are buying new bed linen, there are two systems you might consider. With the hotel system, all the bedding for the entire home is in white or ivory, and so is largely interchangeable, whereas with the family system, each family member has his or her own color of sheets and towels.

LABELS

Sort the remaining linens by person, type or room. Using a permanent laundry pen, mark sheets discreetly by placing a handwritten monogram on the bottom corner of the sheets, if sorting by person, or a single letter indicating bed size (T for twin, D for double, Q for queen, K for king) to sort by type. Then neatly fold and stack back on the shelves.

Many homes have a small linen closet located outside the bathroom that is accessed by the entire family. When this is the case, or if there's a housekeeper making beds and folding sheets and towels, labeling is a must. When everyone knows where things belong, it ensures that items will be put back properly and organization will be maintained.

9 Maintaining order

No one single tip works best when organizing a shared space like the linen closet. Instead, a combination of ideas will help bring order to the chaos.

1 Boxes
Boxes intended for storing clothes under the bed also work well in the linen closet. They can be tucked under shelves and pulled out easily on their wheels.

2 Labeled with love
Reversible crisscrossing elastic bands keep sets of linens together.

3 Perfectly placed
Ordinary bookends and shelf dividers keep rolled or folded washcloths, bath mats and towels stacked neatly.

4 Lining
Fold and stack clean washcloths and towels or pillowcases and sheets in lined baskets, so that they don't get snagged.

5 Personal touch
When organizing drugstore items, group products by user (name of family member) or by category (as you'd shop for them), such as skincare for sunscreens, moisturizers and acne treatment; medications for pain relief, cough, cold, and flu treatments, and allergy medication; and first aid for ointments, thermometer and bandages.

6 Straight and narrow
Learn how to fold items so they lie as flat as possible on the shelf. In thirds is a good method. Fold all linens the same way and stack neatly.

7 Scentsable soaps
Fragranced soaps will perfume a linen closet. Pick a favorite bar and tuck it in the back of the linen closet for your trademark lightly scented bath towels and sheets.

8 Pretty neat
Personalize the individual shelves of each family member by adding a strip of color-coordinated washi tape. It's inexpensive, leaves no residue and can be changed often.

9 High low
Open baskets allow a look at what's inside, while lidded baskets provide a bit of discretion. Position items used most often between hip and eye level; store items used less often above or below.

Craft/hobby space

Decluttering is always time well spent, and that is especially true when organizing craft spaces. Whether you're working from a shoebox or a customized studio, the aim of reorganizing is to keep tools and supplies in sight and accessible, giving you the room to revel in the craft that nourishes your soul.

IT'S ALL ABOUT YOU

Professional organizers are supposed to be objective, but I admit to playing favorites. Among my favorite clients are hobbyists and crafters. They are creative and open-minded, and organizing is an organic process for them, but it doesn't always come naturally. And, here's the best part: the stuff they need to organize is eye candy—scissors shaped like bird beaks; plump pin cushions resembling fruits and vegetables; sparkly beads that make clinking-glass noises as they roll around channeled trays; scraps of textured handmade paper; tubes of paint—you get the idea. Each client's creative space contains layers of mysterious goodies, and each client has a unique process for using them in their art.

There are Pinterest pages, Flickr galleries, websites, magazines and blogs dedicated to organizing studios, workrooms and craft areas for stamping zealots, genealogy buffs, watercolor artists, model railroad enthusiasts and any other indulgence. Some home owners can dedicate a room to their hobby, while for others a space has to be found in another room. The good news is, it is possible to get organized, even if you're working from a tiny tray table. By employing a few organizing principles, you'll be able to get your craft on, even if you need to do it on the kitchen table between meals and homework.

❶ Begin with an epic edit

There's no reason to waste time and money sorting and stashing supplies you are never going to use. Instead, invest time upfront and edit the mess, tossing outdated and unused materials. No more holding onto anything and everything, "just in case." Today is the day to use it or lose it. Search the entire house, and gather all items related to your hobby. With everything laid out in front of you, edit your toolkit and stash, reducing it to items you use.

❷ Sort for you

When fly-tying, do you tie in batches and keep the split tails, thorax flies and woolly buggers

IT TAKES ALL SORTS
Think outside the box when organizing (left and right). Wall-mounted cubbies, wastepaper baskets, tool chests, steamer trunks, test tubes, baby-food jars and trophy cups could all work. Personalize storage with labels, color and style. The store-bought receptacles (right) are from The Container Store.

separate? When designing a necklace, do you select charms and beads by cost, color or size? Organize your materials the way you think you'll use them. Not everyone needs mason jars of color-coordinated embellishments. While yarn looks fluffy and fantastic when color coordinated on shelves, it's not exactly useful if your natural inclination is to look for yarn by type. Instead, it's going to be a frustrating search pawing through each skein of blue, green, yellow and purple to find the blend and weight you're looking for.

❸ Easy access

Be inventive when coming up with storage systems but try to make sure that your out-of-the-box idea is not too far out to be practical. Tall, sturdy, colorful canvas bags with handles hanging from iron hooks on the wall look like a nice solution for fabric storage (it's out of the way), but it's not easily accessible. No one wants to empty a gigantic bag of fabrics to find a specific color for their quilt.

❹ You grow girl!

Allow room for your collection to blossom and bloom. Creative people are inspired frequently to add to their collection of tools and materials. It's human nature to want to think the grass is greener on the other side, and for creative people that means experimenting with new tools of the trade. Leave a little empty space for future creations and purchases. Also, if you move around the house and work in multiple locations, you'll need containers that are portable and fit in the spaces you enjoy working in.

❺ Pick a number—any number

However, don't allow your collection to grow out of control. Every container has a finite amount of space, and a room is simply a container within a home. There must be a point when enough is enough, and putting a stop to shopping is a must! Decide in advance how you'll control inventory and how much space is going to be dedicated to your ikebana addiction. Do you have a small closet that holds 16 shoeboxes of Kenzan flower frogs and pin holders? Or is there only one shelf with room for four boxes? Keep within the limits of your space, and avoid overbuying.

BLANK CANVAS
Decluttering craft supplies instantly improves the look of your "studio" (above left). A small atelier lacks cabinets but makes use of vertical space with the addition of shelves and hooks.

READY FOR ACTION
Craft/hobby storage systems are as unique as the people using them. Every container has potential to stash crafting supplies (above). Purpose-made ribbon dispenser boxes, wicker utensil caddies, glass canisters and even plant pots can be put to good use.

ROUND AND ROUND
Cachepots are used to hold brushes, empty pitchers hold flowers and a wire wastebasket holds cotton canvas rolls.

Packing for vacation

Pack a couple of empty plastic bags to keep for dirty laundry.

Include a second luggage label inside the suitcase.

Split up clothing if traveling with a companion, in case one of your suitcases gets lost in transit.

Pack toiletries inside plastic ziplock bags to prevent liquids from spilling onto clothing.

Don't overpack: ensure you can lift your suitcase up a flight of stairs.

Pack socks inside shoes.

Put heavy items, like shoes, at the bottom of the case, toward the wheels.

Cover shoe soles with shower caps.

Pack clothes that wrinkle inside a dry-cleaning bag before folding to help prevent creases.

For clothes that don't crease, roll rather than folding; you can squeeze more in this way.

Tuck underwear into the empty corners of the case.

Packing for vacation can be stressful and feel complicated. You don't want to pack too much stuff and haul it around, but you are also fearful of not packing something you will need. Having organized closets, bedrooms and bathrooms will make organized packing that much easier, and you can utilize the techniques you have learned as you decluttered your home to streamline your suitcases.

The key to good packing is preparation, so I always advise that you don't leave it to the last minute but give yourself time to feel truly prepared and to get to the store if you realize there are things you need to buy.

LIST IT

Not surprisingly, I also advise using checklists to help you pack efficiently. Categorize the lists and make them relevant to the purpose of your trip and the destination. You can use the checklists on pages 168–169 as they are, or as the basis for your own lists. The same checklists can be used every year for all trips, vacation and pleasure, tweaked, if necessary for different types of destination.

CREATIVE MINIMALISM

There are some creative ways to stretch a wardrobe, which will mean you don't take too many clothes. Stick with solid colors, if possible, and choose items that you can mix and match to create new outfits. Choose easy-care, wrinkle-free fabrics, if possible. Make sure you pack only comfortable, broken-in shoes, and it is a good idea for security reasons to pack costume jewelry rather than your best jewels.

Remember also that you don't have to take everything if items can be easily purchased at your destination.

CHECK THE CASE

Check your luggage as part of the packing process. Luggage can be an expensive investment, so you want to get the most use out of it and utilize the same cases for every trip. Make a note to check that your luggage is suitable for the trip and still in good condition at least a couple of weeks before you plan to leave. When you store your cases, keep in them those items you only use on every trip—travel adaptors, mosquito repellent , toiletries—so they are there when you need them next time.

8 Tips for packing light

Here are some tips to ease the stress of packing and ensure you pack only what you will need and use.

1 Start early
Start the packing process up to a week before you travel, giving you time to gather what you'll need, edit your choices and streamline your suitcases and carry-on bags.

2 Color
Another good way to ensure your wardrobe works well together is to stick to a palette of only two or three colors.

3 Preparation is key
If you are skiing or going to a Caribbean island, you already know what weather conditions to expect and prepare for. For a city break or work trip, you may need to check the weather forecast for the time you will be away in order to make wise clothing choices. You will also need to know what you will be doing—dining out; playing tennis; hiking; meeting clients. Lay out your favorite items for these scenarios. If there is anything in this collection that doesn't have a specific use, don't pack it.

4 Accessorize
All it takes is a few well-chosen accessories to make an outfit work double duty. A necklace, a fancy belt or a pretty scarf can turn daywear into evening chic.

5 Divide and conquer
With everything laid out in front of you, edit your choices by one-third, or even half. Baggage fees can make flying very expensive; be ruthless. How many times have you packed four pairs of shorts but only worn two?

6 Go natural
Edit your toiletry choices as you would edit your clothes. It's easier to go natural on vacation, so you won't be needing all your everyday makeup.

7 Capsule
Make sure everything you pack will get used by preparing a mini vacation capsule wardrobe (see Closets, pages 82–87). Think about complete outfits, and make sure every item of clothing will work with other items in the bag: if your patterned blouse can't be worn with at least two other pieces, don't pack it.

8 Wear heavy
Can you wear your heaviest or bulkiest clothes on the journey? Instead of packing your ski jacket, wear it.

DIGITAL
CLUTTER

03

Organizing our digital lives can be more daunting than physically decluttering our homes, but the peace of mind that comes from doing so will have the same positive outcome: being able to find what you need, when you need it.

Electronic files

t's not unusual to have what feels like zillions of emails and electronic files to keep track of and process. Email is probably the most-used software program there is, but what should be a time saver can quite easily become a time thief.

TAKE BACK CONTROL

To start taking control of your email, think of it as you would snail-mail: flyers and junk mail is tossed; mail needing action, like a bill, is put in your tickler file; letters and packages are read and kept, as appropriate. You can deal with emails in exactly the same way.

First, choose specific times daily to tackle emails, perhaps twice each day (see Prioritizing: Turn Off the Tech, see page 127). Scan the inbox for junk and spam, and delete these without opening them. Speed-read subject lines, and move irrelevant and unimportant messages to the trash. If, later that week, you realize you need that email, retrieve it from the trash. Empty the trash once or twice a month, on schedule. Only after you've reduced your inbox to only relevant messages should you begin to read the priority mail.

PROCESSING

Processing emails is the act of responding to or organizing messages for future attention. During your designated email time, if you can reply to an email in less then just a few minutes, then go straight ahead and do it. Then file the email (see Filing, below). To process emails that will take longer, you will need to prioritize by considering factors of importance, urgency and what you would like to do (see Prioritizing: Grading Your Priorities, see page 127)

The last emails are those that require input from others, or that cannot be responded to until another task is completed. To clear these from your inbox, put them in a folder labeled Pending or separate them further using folders labeled Action Needed and Awaiting Reply. Check these folders as part of your email processing routine, to see if further actions can be taken.

FILING

Email messages in your inbox can be deflating and distracting, so use a system of folders to manage them. As with home filing (see pages 92–94), keep your categories broad, and give each folder a name that tells you what it contains at a glance. Your folders might be categorized by:
- **Actions required** Respond; Follow-up; Research—remember to check these folders regularly, as action will be required.
- **Stage of project** Pending, Due, Done, Future—again, check these folders regularly, since action may be required.
- **Topic** Receipts, Registrations, Travel.
- **Contact name** (last name first with hyphen) Churchill-Winston.
- **Project type** Organizing; subcategories: Org_closets, Org_collectibles.

MINCE WORDS

Email overload wears everyone out, so think about using email only when necessary. If you had to photocopy and stamp snail mail what you are about to send via email, would you still do it? The jokes and one-line thank you's are unnecessary. Don't send them; don't respond to them.

- **Use as few words as possible** Write in telegraph form when communicating casually with "regulars." For example, "Got your email; will respond in detail later." Or, "Kids are sick. Can't make it tonight; see you next month." Obviously, there are times when this is inappropriate, but use it when you can.

- **In a nutshell** Try to make emails "previewable" so that readers don't have to open the email or respond to it. If you can, fit the message on the subject line, headline style, so recipients know there is no need to click it open. For example, "Cupcakes were a hit; we raised $500!" If you need to impart more information, implement a no-scroll rule, with everything on one screen. Send longer materials as an attachment that the recipient knows they can come back to when they have the time.

- **First things** Start the email by stating what you want the reader to know and do: "Deadline to sign up for book fair is tonight; Tuesday and Thursday shifts still available."

- **Reuse content sent repeatedly** Not every email needs to be made from scratch; it's OK to "reheat" content for similar messages sent to different recipients. The orientation leader sending a "Welcome New Members" email need only tweak generic content to make each message personal.

MANAGING ELECTRONIC FILES

In the good old days, before email, there were "hard" copies printed on paper. These days, however, we are under pressure to go paperless and use only electronic files, so we have to find a way to keep and manage important information safe, organized and easily accessible. Using these

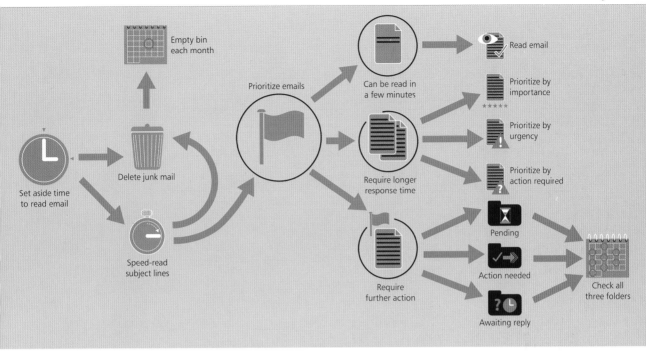

tips will help you tame the digital dragons and manage your personal files and folders.

■ **Sort by YYYYMMDD** If you are a parent-helper in your third-grader's school and you need to send notes to parents, you could create a year-long stream of "Notes to Parents" files and keep them in date order, like, "Notes to Parents Feb 7," "Notes to Parents Feb 14," and so on. Get into the habit of using a four-digit year, followed by a two-digit month and a two-digit day, like "Note to Parents 2015-02-07." When you include the date, your computer will sort like-named files in chronological order. The work is done for you. Do not use single digits alone. Start one-digit numbers with zero (such as 01, 02); otherwise, the computer will order the files 1, 10, 11, 2, 20, 3, and so on, instead of 1, 2, 3, 10, 11, 20.

■ **Include version numbers in file names** When writing drafts, include revision or version numbers. If the weekly notes to parents require multiple approvals before sending, there needs to be a system in place for keeping track of the latest version to ensure an incorrect copy is not sent. If the teacher reviews the note and makes changes, the new version should be renamed by adding "v02" to the end of the file name. If it is read by someone else who needs to approve it, make the changes and rename it "v03." This method shows in an instant which document is the most up to date.

■ **File your folders** Files, clearly labeled using the tips above, are stored in folders, much like they would be in a conventional paper filing system. You might start with a broad category, and label a folder "Organization." Soon, however, your folder fills up with a wide range of information on vaguely related organizational topics. Within the parent folder "Organization," include folders that narrow down choices and make it easy for you to find what you need: ORGANIZATION_**Check-Lists**, ORGANIZATION_**DIY-Ideas**, ORGANIZATION_**Expert-Advice**. Within these folders, further subcategories can be included to help you find your files quickly and easily.

NAMING FILES AND FOLDERS

Use these labeling ideas to make finding your files and folders a stress-free task.

■ Personal names are easier to locate if you label family name first, followed by first name or initials.
■ When it comes to capitalizing words or phrases, there are several options, but keeping it as simple as possible means using a cap for the first letter of each word— CamelCapsFile.xxx.
■ Go from general to specific, so "Gardening_ Flowers_Perrenial_Shade_ White_LilyoftheValley' rather than "White_ Flowers_Gardening."

Digital photographs

Now that cameras in phones are ubiquitous, we can store thousands of photos and spread them across multiple devices and storage systems. The number of digital photographs we're hoarding is staggering. For the average user, finding, viewing, editing, sharing and safely storing these photos is complicated. While there's no picture-perfect solution that will appeal to everyone, there are tips that will help the typical user understand what needs to be done to organize and safely store digital photos, using a combination of at least one online and one offline solution.

WHAT TO DO

Begin by gathering every camera, phone and SD (Security Digital) memory card. For those who have never paid attention, it's worth noting that when photos come from different sources they may have different file names: DSC (Nikon); IMG (Canon); SAM (Samsung). Another surprise is that it's not uncommon to discover you have hundreds of stored photos.

- **Look** View every photo through two lenses: that of a critical curator and that of an armchair psychologist. Think about what you're keeping, why you're keeping it and how many are worth keeping. It's better to have six decent photos that can be quickly accessed instead of six dozen that you haven't bothered viewing, editing, labeling or organizing and can't find when you need them.
- **Tag** Name or tag each photo, using some of the advice given on pages 118–119. When putting photographs in folders, keep the category names simple and consistent. Generic tags, such as Vacations, Family, Nature, Food and Birthdays work well. Both Mac and Window systems limit characters, including the file extensions (JPG or RAW) to 260 characters, so be concise when naming and tagging. Use underscores or dashes but not other characters to name files.
- **Geo-tagging** While geo-tagging helps pre-sort photos and prevents them from getting

mixed up in other albums, it harbors a security concern. Geo-tagging embeds a location where the photo was taken, and if the photos are posted online, the exact location can be discerned. Parents who post photos of their children may not want the photo location revealed. Geo-tagging is the default setting on most phones and photo-organizing apps. You may choose to turn off this feature.

COPIES

When it comes to photos, one storage solution is not enough, so keep your photos on an external and a cloud solution.

Cloud services are online, which means that if the Internet isn't available, neither are your photographs. This isn't the case with external hard drives, which have the software that can perform scheduled, one-click and click-free backups. All you do is plug it into your computer and it finds all of your important files. It's fast and has oodles of storage. Digital pack rats rejoice knowing they can download and store photos, music, movies and TV shows without running out of storage, and large-capacity external hard drives are affordable. Some external hard drives are like "private clouds," allowing users to access files anywhere, even while away from home.

Cloud storage protects data from local threats, such as fire, flood and power surges, so can be used in conjunction with a hard drive. With cloud services you can access all of your backed-up documents or media from any Internet-connected computer, tablet or smartphone in the world. You can also use it to share your photos. Instead of emailing large photo or video files that take forever to download, store them in the cloud, send a link and let the recipient download them. It's quick and convenient and keeps the inbox tidy.

CONSIDERATION
Take some time to choose the photographs that are worth keeping, and don't be afraid to delete others.

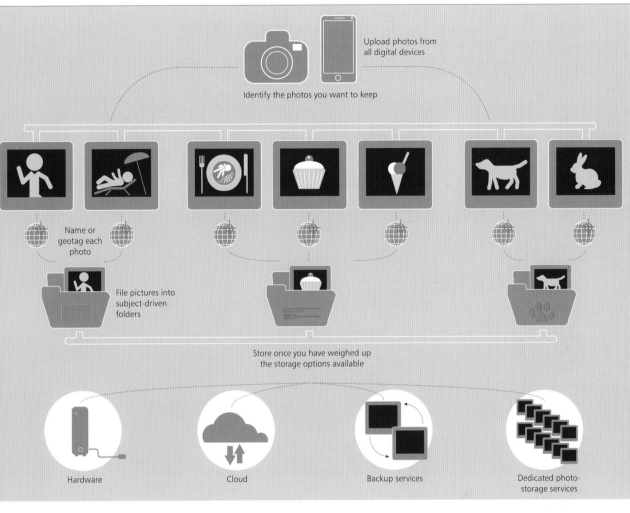

Upload photos from all digital devices

Identify the photos you want to keep

Name or geotag each photo

File pictures into subject-driven folders

Store once you have weighed up the storage options available

Hardware | Cloud | Backup services | Dedicated photo-storage services

SORTING DIGITAL PHOTOGRAPHS
Once photos are edited and sorted, it is far more likely that you will be able to find images that you want.

BACKUP SERVICES
Explore options for keeping separate copies of data in more than one place. Many backup services are "set it and forget it": They work silently, and you don't have to do a thing. Backup services are helpful in the event your computer crashes or is stolen. Choose the extent of backup right for you. Backblaze, for instance, backs up your entire Mac, while Flickr simply holds your photos and is considered a second-tier backup.

DEDICATED PHOTO-STORAGE SERVICES
If you want to edit, organize and share photos, you'll want to upload them to a dedicated photo-storage and sharing site. Some require you to manually upload files; others offer automatic uploads from your phone to your storage site. Some require more advanced tech skills. When choosing a photo-share service, consider the following:

- Who controls the privacy settings for photo collections?
- Does the service mine your data or add advertising?
- Is information backed-up and/or encrypted?
- Who retains ownership of images?
- How much does it cost? Is it renewed automatically?
- Are organizing and editing features available?
- What are the photo-sharing options?
- Are there file size limitations? (Important for scanned items, printed photos, digital video and digitized data from phones and cameras.)
- Can full-resolution photos be preserved in any size, without compression?
- Is it possible to create products (books, calendars and prints)?
- What methods are available for organizing albums? (By date, theme or face recognition?)

Digital decluttering

DAILY

○ **Back up**
Use an automatic backup program. A second, external backup is optional.

○ **Update contacts**
Immediately change phone numbers, email addresses or physical addresses when you receive updates.

○ **Process emails**
See page 118.

○ **Purge downloads folder**
Immediately save and store downloads for keeping in an appropriate location, other than the downloads folder.

WEEKLY

○ **Declutter the desktop**
End each working week by tidying up your desktop and putting documents, images and downloads where they belong (trash or folders). If items on your desktop are awaiting information, follow up on the answers you need; if you need to take action on the items on your desktop, take care of them now or schedule time on your calendar for those actions.

○ **Virus scanning**
Particularly for PCs, make sure virus scanning software is up to date. Run a full scan.

○ **Operating system, software and app updates**
For any updates not set to install automatically, do a quick scan to find anything new, determine if you want that update and, if so, take time to properly and completely install it.

○ **Tidy projects and tasks**
For example, project management tools and to-do lists.

○ **Delete call history**
Your mobile phone is a data mine of information about you. Delete old messages.

○ **Trash**
Just as you take out the household trash for weekly collection, empty the trash on each of your laptops and desktop computers.

○ **Clear browser history and cache**
Your computer's browser history is a log of all websites you visit, while the cache keeps a copy of the pages so that you can revisit them quickly. Delete both on all desktop computers, laptops and mobile devices.

○ **Clean exteriors**
Clean screens and monitors and sanitize keyboards and mobile devices to keep them fresh and healthy. Use an air duster to clean between keys.

○ **Disable cookies**
This is a personal preference. Some people like cookies (digital flags that tell what sites you've visited and allow advertisers to compile a picture of you), others don't want ads popping up. Disable cookies or enable "private browsing" before shopping or researching personal products. Otherwise, a site you visited might appear in an ad in a sidebar when you least expect it.

Digital decluttering doesn't need to be done in a day. Like other housekeeping chores, a few tasks should be done daily, while others can be done weekly or seasonally.

SEASONAL: AT LEAST TWICE YEARLY

○ **Information management**
Failure to properly filter information and harvest the keepers leads to an overdose on research findings, articles, blog posts, e-newsletters and typed notes. Streamline the information several times per year.

○ **Images, photos, music, movies**
Images (the logo or photo of your realtor that you don't want to save but ends up on your hard drive anyway), photos (the pictures you take and possibly want to save), and music and movies don't have to live on your computer forever. Delete them or store (see pages 120–121).

○ **Delete mobile phone apps**
Delete obsolete apps, or ones you no longer use.

○ **Delete document files**
Search for and delete obsolete files.

○ **Document sharing**
If you're no longer collaborating on a project, delete the shared folder associated with it. Make sure that others have access and permission to make changes first. If you need to keep it, for use as a template for later projects, store it (see pages 118–119).

○ **Tidy texts**
Delete meaningless or out-of-date text messages, sent, received and draft.

○ **Update passwords**
Passwords should be updated several times a year; at the very minimum, change them annually.

○ **Purge social media**
When you've had enough of your frenemies' bragging, complaining or self-promoting, it's time to de-friend, unlike, uncircle, unfollow and unsubscribe. For pages posting too often, remove notifications; alternatively, if you really like what a page is sharing, make sure to add a notification for each time it posts.

○ **Uninstall programs that aren't being used.**

SET IT AND FORGET IT

Put these tasks on autopilot

○ Firewalls

○ Disk cleanup (built into PC; Disk Doctor for Mac).

○ Quick virus scan weekly; full virus scan monthly

○ Disk defragmentation for PCs; not necessary for Macs.

○ Installing updates: Many are automatic, but on some systems, you'll want to manually check every week.

CALENDAR CLUTTER

04

If your calendar is cluttered and bursting with appointments and activities, and no white space is put aside for enjoying life, then you are overworked, overstressed and over committed. In this chapter we look at how you and the members of your household can easily organize each and every day, so that life becomes more productive, calm and enjoyable.

Prioritizing

There's more to being organized than living with less stuff, acquiring less stuff and sorting or categorizing stuff. Truly organized people purposefully plan how they'll spend their money, energy and time. This means not mechanically accepting invites, tasks or duties. When it comes to not cluttering calendars, we need to make conscious decisions that will enable us to manage what we do with our time in an attempt to live a less rushed and less stressful life. To do this we need to manage our commitments, activities and tasks. What we are really talking about is deciding what's most important. Learning to prioritize is the secret to annihilating calendar clutter.

PRIORITIZING YOUR TIME

Time management is about managing what we do with our time. We are familiar with other management systems, such as weight management. We know that if we exercise portion control of what we eat, we will gradually change physically. The same is true when we exercise portion control when making commitments, such as booking appointments, accepting invitations, attending meetings, signing kids up for activities and socializing. We need to control the portion sizes so they are manageable and our calendar becomes leaner.

This is where decluttering comes in. Just as your home becomes more organized through decluttering, so can your calendar.

Ways to manage and prioritize your time include creating daily routines and weekly plans (see pages 130–131), discussing them with the members of the household (see pages 132–133) and learning to say "no" to unimportant activities (see pages 128–129), allowing you to do everything that needs to be done in a calm manner, and even leave time over for just enjoying life.

PRIORITIZING TASKS

By creating and clarifying goals, staying focused and prioritizing and managing tasks, we clear our calendars of clutter and spend time with intention. Actively choosing which tasks to tackle when is the key to task management.

There are typically two camps on this topic. Camp Big Rocks is of the mindset that the most onerous tasks get tackled first, while the opposing camp believes that starting with the done-in-five-minutes-or-less tasks is the way to go.

If you prefer to "get it over and done with," then starting with the larger task could be a good choice. That way, once the big task is completed you can "treat" yourself with the smaller, lighter, less-dreaded tasks.

Alternatively, deciding to check multiple, smaller items off the to-do list could be the boost you need to get your momentum going, and, once in motion, you tend to stay in motion. You will find that checking items off the list motivates you to keep going, and when it's time for bigger tasks, you've "snacked" on the smaller stuff, but are now ready for the main course.

The third process (let's call it Camp Combo) uses a combination of each system, depending on what needs to

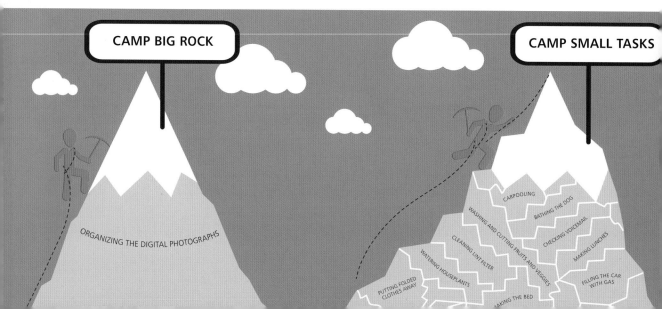

> 66 Learning to prioritize is the secret to annihilating calendar clutter. 99

be done, the time you have available and how you are feeling. Does your to-do list include small stuff like moving emails into the junk folder or changing a password? Or do you need to accomplish larger tasks that require more time? Mastering your schedule is about making savvy decisions based on time constraints, fluctuations in your energy and concentration, life circumstances and time of the year (see Grading Your Priorities, right).

FLEXIBILITY
There's a lot to be said for trusting that what feels right in the summer might not be a good fit for winter. As the outside world and the vagaries of life impose distractions, opportunities and demands, even the best planners and schedulers succumb to the complexities and never-ending developmental changes of, perhaps, a toddler having a tantrum, or a health challenge forcing a shift in priorities. At these times, knowing when to postpone actions or delegate tasks to others is mindful and purposeful.

TURN OFF THE TECH
While technological advances like email, voicemail and texting are convenient, for many they may be more harmful than helpful when it comes to managing our time. These tools have exacerbated our workloads by allowing us to access anyone, anytime, and other people assume we are always wired, waiting and ready to respond.

To take back control of your time you need to know when to turn off the tech. Once you have prioritized and made a commitment to a task, give it your full attention to ensure it is carried out productively and enjoyably.

As part of your daily routine, having set times to deal with emails and calls not only helps you get on with the activities you have prioritized, but also helps to manage other people's expectations of you. Once they get the idea that you will read and address emails or texts at one of, say, four times each day, they won't expect you to drop everything when they send you a message or give you a call.

These tips for working out what is important work in conjunction with each other. Write down every task and consider each, grading it by these categories, then use those grades in combination to help you figure out what should be done when.

1 Time
How long will the activity or task take? Do I have time for that? Is there a deadline? When you write it all down, you get a much better idea of what can be done at any particular time. If you need your work uniform ironed for tomorrow, then prioritize this ahead of tidying the pantry. When you know you only have ten minutes available, you can check off a quick task, and save more time-consuming tasks for later. A word of warning here: be realistic about how much time you will need.

2 Importance
Which tasks or activities are most important, and why? This is a matter of personal relevance. You may decide to look at the consequences of not completing the task or attending the activity to rank order of importance, or consider how whether you do or don't accept an invitation will impact on the invitee—will your best friend be mortified, or will your son's friend's mom not even notice you aren't there?

3 Exertion/concentration required
Consider how much energy or concentration each task or activity will require. If you know you won't have the energy to fully appreciate a yoga class that starts straight after work, then don't sign up for it. If you know your energy levels are at their highest straight after breakfast, then make a note that this is a good time to start decluttering the garage.

4 Worst first
In conjunction with the previous considerations, grade your list of tasks and priorities by order of enjoyment, then decide if you should tackle your least favorite job first, or build up to it by tackling some of the easier chores.

CAMP COMBO

CREATING A FILING SYSTEM
BATHING THE DOG
WASHING WINDOWS
PACKING FOR VACATION
SHREDDING JUNK MAIL
DISCARDING LEFTOVERS FROM FRIDGE
DEFROSTING THE FREEZER
PLANNING DINNERS FOR THE WEEK
ORGANIZING PHOTOS
TAKING OUT THE TRASH AND RECYCLING
MAKING THE BED
WATERING HOUSE

I have another commitment.

I'm currently in the middle of several other projects.

I'm unavailable that day.

Saying "NO"

Chic, upscale shopping boutiques have an "airy" feel. There's typically a lot of empty space—not wasted space, but free space. In the store there's plenty of aisle space between racks of clothing. Hanging rails are kept sparse and piles of folded clothes kept compact. Savvy boutique owners hand-select the best items for their pampered shoppers and strategically place only a few at a time out for purchase. On their websites there's intentionally much less clutter in the margins, headers and footers. There's a feeling of exclusivity created by purposefully leaving "white space" around featured objects. That "less is more" look is a very effective way to capture attention. It forces us to notice featured items. It's calming and feels luxe.

The same is true for our calendars. When we do more, we enjoy less. When we leave white space on our calendars, we allow ourselves to enjoy aspects of life that we may otherwise be missing out on. White space also enables us to productively and effectively approach the necessary activities and tasks. And the key to creating white space on a calendar is the ability to say "no."

OUT OF OPERATION

When your calendar has no white space, you will inevitably find yourself mindlessly trawling through appointments like a hamster on a wheel, every day packed so full of "things to do" that no day is special or unique. You have no time left to "stop and smell the roses," to enjoy meaningful conversations.

Parents often have a desire to do simple, ordinary, spontaneous things with their children, but opportunities are missed amid a whirlwind of scheduled activities. This stressful existence means you neglect the people you care about and you don't practice self-care. To start giving yourself time to enjoy life, establish hours of operation, making sure you leave time free when you are not officially "operating" in the service of others. During the "off" times, remember to disconnect electronically in order to really connect with friends, family and yourself.

WHAT STAYS, AND WHAT GOES?

Create a list of priorities and goals to help you decide which activities are worthy of your time and attention, and learn to say "no" to everything else. Are there unimportant things that can be unscheduled? If so, then go ahead and unschedule. Find ways to say "no" when asked to participate in optional events. Say "no" to holiday parties that aren't going to bring joy and happiness. Say "no" to volunteering for charities that you aren't passionate about. Say "yes" to empty space on your calendar, knowing that it is not wasted space.

SAY "NO" WITHOUT SAYING "NO"

If saying "no" is a no-no in your vocabulary, work on ideas for ways to say it gently, without actually saying the word. For example:

> I'm not in a position to bake cupcakes. But I am happy to donate toward the cause.

> Please ask someone else to take a turn and step up.

> I don't have the time.

- "I'm not in a position to bake 13 dozen cupcakes; I can donate $20 toward the purchase, though, if that would help?"
- "I prefer you ask someone else to take a turn and step up. I've been doing this for two seasons."
- "I have another commitment."
- "I'm in the middle of several other projects with pending deadlines."
- "I'm unavailable that (night, day, weekend)."

You can also use your calendar to buy you some time to come up with a suitable response. Tell the person that you need to check your calendar and you will get back to them once you have done so, giving you a chance to formulate a more thoughtful response.

EXIT STRATEGY
Friends, family and colleagues occasionally send invitations where saying "no" isn't an option. For these functions it's important to have a start and finish time in mind for a polite visit. There's no need to be the first to arrive or the last to leave.

Figuring out how to disengage and exit gracefully is difficult in social situations, so, before arriving, create a farewell line and deliver it upon greeting the host. "I'm happy I could attend, although I regret I'll need to leave early," or "I better get busy mixing and mingling since my time is limited," or "Thanks so much for putting this together; I can only stay a few minutes, but I'll follow up with a call next week."

3 Ways with distractions

With the best will in the world, if you find the white space you have gifted yourself is interrupted, you need to find ways to say "no" to these distractions from your time. The best way to do this is to manage other people's expectations on your time.

1 Rearrange
When someone calls or stops by to talk about an unplanned topic, ask them if they can wait until (date, time of your choice) because you're busy with something else at the moment. After a few times, they'll get the hint that you mean business and will respect your time.

2 On your terms
Establish times for responding to voicemails and stick to them—don't use your white-space time to respond. Let everyone know when they can expect a response by including an indication in your outgoing voicemail message—for example "Please leave a message. I typically reply to voicemails after 3pm on the day the message is left."

3 Get to the point
To avoid getting into lengthy, unnecessary chats that eat into your time, prioritize conversations by starting with the most important topic. For example, "Myra, I've only got a few minutes, but I can confirm that I will pick up Allison from Granville Tower on Friday afternoon. I'll text her when I'm in the parking lot."

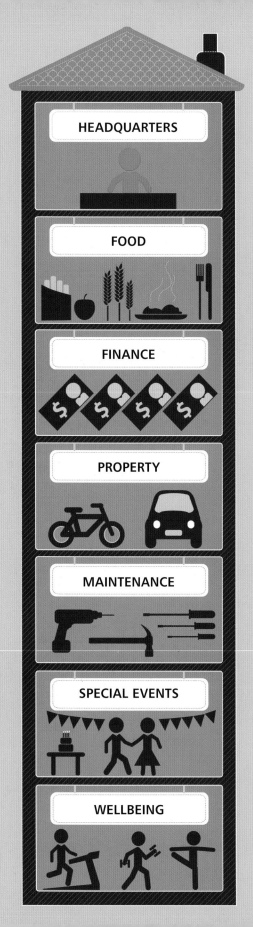

Embrace routines

Most people don't approach running their home like running a business, but essentially that's what they are doing. Think of home as headquarters and managing it and everyone in it as a career. The job description includes overseeing multiple departments: food (menu planning, grocery shopping, meal preparation); finance (insurance, investments, taxes, banking); property (home, cars, bikes); maintenance (housekeeping); special events (vacations, birthdays); and "thrive" (wellbeing—physical, emotional, spiritual, behavioral). Keeping all these departments spinning smoothly requires patience, creativity, discipline, spontaneity, sensitivity, structure and routines.

DAILY ROUTINES

Routines help families transform hectic into harmonious by morphing certain behaviors into comfortable habits. For example, the act of brushing your teeth and putting the toothbrush back in the same place, near the sink where it's used every day, is a habit that is so ingrained that we do it without thinking about it.

Anyone desperate for a more organized life should consider creating a few simple routines. Having certain routines in place will make everyday transitions less stressful. Mornings are a great example. On a work or school day, getting out of the house on time can be particularly stressful. All family members need to be cleaned, dressed, fed and packed off with bags containing their provisions for the day. Achieving this feat without a routine that all household members are aware of and adhere to can turn the morning into a manic, stressful, rushed affair that starts the day in a bad way. Consider what everyone needs to achieve before they leave the house and build the necessary tasks into a morning routine. Perhaps everyone will get dressed before breakfast, and clean teeth straight after breakfast. This routine will soon become habit; it will happen without anyone thinking about it.

A streamlined morning routine may benefit from a few pre-bedtime routines. Perhaps school bags should be packed with the books needed for the next day before the bedtime bath, while making the packed lunches after dinner and before you relax for the evening could go some way toward making mornings more enjoyable and stress free.

SECURITY IN STRUCTURE
The structure of daily routines helps us to master small tasks so that we can take control of bigger, unpredictable things with confidence. Many parents set a bedtime routine for their children, such as a warm bath, a short story, a tuck-in and a kiss goodnight. A predictable bedtime routine signals to children that they are safe and cared for, which results in them falling asleep and staying asleep.

WEEKLY PLANNING

Planning is key to a less stressful home life, because with a plan in place everyone knows what is expected of them. You will already have a weekly routine that revolves around work hours, school and regular activities such as an evening class or your children's sports practice or drama club. Each week there will be extra activities added to that routine, such as dental appointments or a birthday party, and tasks that need to be accomplished, such as buying a card and present to take to the party. Establishing what these extras are each week will ensure that everyone knows what they have to do and when, and allows you to plan ahead for them, which will make the week run that bit more smoothly.

A family meeting (see pages 132–133) is the perfect forum for making the weekly plan. Find out who has what additions to the normal routine and establish who this affects and how. Then plan for those activities as required.

Detail the activities on the calendar (see pages 134–135) and make sure everyone is aware of how this impacts them, writing down specific details if necessary.

5 Planning ahead

Knowing what to expect for the week ahead keeps you organized, but can also save you time, money and stress.

1 Meal plan
Planning your meals for the week saves time, money and waste. Plan the meals in relation to what is happening that week, then shop only for what you need for those meals. If you know that everyone will be late home on Tuesday, choose a quick dinner for that night, such as a pizza from the freezer that requires no effort from tired family members.

2 Chore plan
Certain tasks need to be carried out every week, such as making packed lunches or walking the dog. Using a chore plan, you can assign chores to family members, and yourself, based around the existing activities they have that week.

3 Planning to multitask
Look at your weekly plan and recognize times when you may be dormant or in limbo—for example, while traveling on a train, waiting for a flight or sitting in the car while your child has soccer practice. Establish activities that can be completed during these times, perhaps replying to emails on your smartphone or even gifting yourself the time to read a novel.

4 Weekly checklist
This is a more open plan of things that can be done this week if there is time. Write a list of the tasks you hope to achieve, but don't be a slave to it; simply pick out a task when you have the opportunity, and tick it off.

5 Bundle tasks
When reviewing your weekly routine, consider bundling all the small tasks that are normally spread out during the week. This is an efficient and satisfying way to save time and keep you focused on matters at hand.

Family meetings

amily meetings not only keep calendar chaos to a minimum, they reduce stress, unite the family as a team, teach kids how to solve problems, reinforce family culture and give everyone in the family a chance to be heard and validated.

Family meetings are useful for anyone who needs to take control of their time, whether that be a couple with a busy work and social schedule that doesn't seem to leave time for shopping, laundry or tidying the house; a single-parent family juggling transport to after-school activities and access with the other parent; or a family with both parents living under the same roof but somehow never managing to get the kids to their destination on time or find the time to get the dishes washed and the dog walked.

MAKING MEETINGS WORK
Frantic-free families use face-to-face family meetings to minimize stress and maximize communication. Scheduled, on-the-calendar family gatherings are where the seeds of

organization are planted, but be patient; it takes years for seeds to root and sprout. There will be meetings where the sun shines or it pours rain and topics become slippery slopes. But one thing is for sure: navigating family meetings season after season has its benefits.

As well as the opportunity to review the calendars of all members of the household and plan for the week ahead (see pages 130–131) you will have a chance to discuss household chores that can be carried out to keep the home in order. On top of this, family meetings teach children the importance of belonging and wanting to contribute to the family and to society. Parents want their kids to become civilized, respectful, happy and well-adjusted people who enjoy the company of others and live a pleasant, peaceful life, and family meetings can impart these values from an early age. Held regularly, these meetings become a port-in-a-storm for the tumultuous teen years. No one is barking orders or criticizing; it's a time when order and calm are the norm and family business is discussed.

MEETING POINT
Getting the family together at the same time each week allows everyone to review their activities and plan for the week ahead.

11 Tips for productive family meetings

To make the most of your time and keep stress levels low, here are some tips to ensure that your family meetings are of use to everyone.

1 Keep it regular
Aim to have a meeting once a week, preferably at the same time each week so that no one can claim they didn't know anything about it.

2 Attend
Once you've found a time, announce it to the family, along with your expectation that everyone honor it. Everything else needs to be scheduled around the family meeting.

3 Attend means paying attention
Remind that mental as well as physical attendance is required. No gaming, no texting, no answering the phone during meetings.

4 Be punctual
To set the tone for the meeting and lead by example it is important that the leader or co-leaders are punctual.

5 Review calendar appointments
A good way to start the meeting is to discuss everyone's appointments for the coming week, including pets. Make sure the appointments are detailed on the family calendar (see pages 134–135).

6 Take the lead
Decide who is going to lead or co-lead the meeting. In single-parent households, this isn't a problem—the adult leads—but in families with two parents living under the same roof, one parent leads, or the parents act as co-leaders, or take turns planning and executing meetings.

7 Delegate
Discuss the feasibility of when the mundane tasks of everyday life can be realistically achieved in light of the coming week's calendar commitments. Confirm who will be responsible, assigning age-appropriate responsibilities and tasks to all members of the household.

8 Announcements and agendas
Some families like to write discussion points on a white board, create an electronic agenda or have a paper-and-pencil outline. Once you start having meetings regularly, you'll notice things throughout the week that you and others want to discuss. Add these items to the agenda as they occur. Stick to points on the agenda, and respect everyone's time and attention.

9 Review who's responsible
Leading on from the above tip, simply stating what's coming up doesn't always translate into actionable items. Sometimes people have trouble sequencing events. To clarify doubts, it's important to point out what's scheduled, what's expected, who's responsible and what are the deadlines. For example, "Caroline, you have an away-soccer game on Wednesday afternoon. You'll need to pack a snack and make sure your uniform is washed and ready the night before. Rachel, this means you need to feed the dog and take out the trash on Wednesday since Caroline won't be home until after 9pm. She'll repay the favor the following week."

10 Find a time
Arrange the meeting for a time that suits everyone, when no one will be tired and irritable or clock-watching because they have somewhere else to be. Find a day and time when each family member can give their full attention to the meeting, and impart the importance of putting the details in diaries or on calendars. Be flexible, be inclusive and be respectful of what's on everyone's agenda—but at the same time promote the understanding that this is not a casual arrangement, but a commitment.

11 Follow through
Actions speak louder than words. Modeling the behaviors discussed during meetings is mandatory. For example, if one of the goals is to have less rushed, less chaotic mornings, parents need to practice what's preached and implement before-bed routines themselves (see page 130).

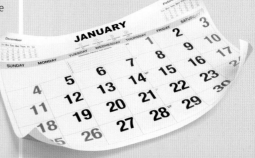

The household calendar

In order to schedule and organize your time using the methods discussed so far, you need a calendar. Having appointments and commitments all carefully detailed in one place where everyone can see it allows you to ascertain where you have time available to schedule in something new, or whether you need to say "no" and give yourself a little free time. The calendar is essential to weekly planning and is a reminder to all in the household of where they might need to be or what they might need to do.

CALENDAR FORMATS

There are various calendar formats to consider, so spend time analyzing what type of calendar will be most suitable for your lifestyle. It boils down to the needs of the particular household. If separated parents share custody of children, both adults benefit from being able to access information related to sporting events and school vacations, but they don't need access to each other's personal calendars.

The first consideration is whether you prefer a wall calendar, desk system or electronic organizer. Wall options include paper, dry-erase or chalkboard versions. The chalkboard and dry-erase systems are great for weekly planning, but you will also need another system to record information further ahead in time.

If you need a portable format, then a diary, download-and-print or electronic system that syncs to your smartphone could be a good choice. If considering download and print, don't forget to take ink costs into consideration. With electronic systems, you can set up recurring events, such as birthdays or a weekly commitment, and reminders.

LAYOUT OPTIONS

As well as format, consider which layout option is most suited to your needs. Calendars may be organized monthly, weekly or daily; be dated or undated (user fills in dates); feature columns or blocks for appointments, or lines; have preprinted time slots or remain blank for you to fill in yourself; include time increments; and have a start day of Monday or Sunday. Some diaries, planners and calendars also have space for recording extra information, such as to-do or shopping lists, and may also have pockets in which to place pieces of information relevant to that month.

With paper systems, whether wall or desk, consider the amount of space available for writing in relation to how much information you are likely to record. Do you need separate sections for various members of the household? With electronic systems you can modify layout views in numerous ways.

CHOOSING A CALENDAR LAYOUT
There are several layout options to consider when choosing a calendar. Two of the most important considerations are how far ahead you need to see with one glance and how much you need to write on.

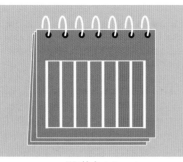

Weekly layout

Monthly layout

Yearly layout

5 Keeping the calendar efficient

It's tempting to blame a habitual lack of punctuality or missed appointments on your calendar, but calendars are just another tool, and you remain in control of it. To ensure that it is efficient and up to date, you must use the calendar properly, and make sure that everyone else in the household also adheres to these calendar rules.

1 Date and time
The purpose of keeping a calendar is to effectively handle date- and time-specific commitments. If it isn't date specific, put it on a note IN but not ON your calendar, so that you can move it around as other demands take priority.

2 Set reminders
If you use an electronic calendar system, set up reminders to give you warning of an upcoming event. Make sure you set the reminder enough time in advance to prepare for the appointment, whether that be 30 minutes to drive there, or a week ahead to schedule a time to buy a birthday gift and card.

3 Visit the calendar
There is no point in recording your comings and goings if you then don't refer back to them. Check the calendar daily and make plans for the next day if necessary.

4 Write it down right away
Add appointments to the calendar as soon as you make them, and always refer to the calendar when scheduling new appointments to avoid clashes.

5 Leave the pen
Keep a pen always with the calendar or planner, and make sure everyone knows it must not be removed.

USE IT WELL
No matter what format it takes, or where it is housed, a calendar is only efficient if everyone uses it correctly. With all the information recorded on the calendar, all members of the household are "in the know."

maandag	dinsdag	woensdag	donderdag	vrydag	saterdag	sondag	
⭐	1	2	3	4	5	6	januarie
							februarie
							maart
7	8 10:00 Tandarts	9	10	11 KAMP	12 KAMP	13 KAMP	april
							mei
14	15	16	17	18	19 Kobus 40ste 17:00	20	junie
							julie
21	22	23	24 18:00 Klara Skool konsert	25	26	27	augustus
							september
							oktober
28	29	30	31		• Geskenk Susan • DSTV • Max vakansie		november
							desember

The administration station

A time-saving administration station is an extension of the household calendar. It includes pieces of useful information that can be quickly accessed when needed. It ensures that everyone in the household is kept in the know and is an area within a home that helps members of a household facilitate clear communication. A couple with conflicting work patterns whose paths don't cross as often as they might like, or a busy, active family can benefit from setting up their own administration station where they know they can find a particular piece of information.

SINGULAR SENSATION

You should have one, and only one, administration station, set up in a spot that all members of the household can access easily. It might be in the same place as the household calendar. It can take the form of a single binder with plastic sleeves, a box containing a diary, address book and notebook, or wall-mounted baskets or clear pockets.

WHAT TO INCLUDE

What you keep in the administration station is down to you, whatever information is most useful and asked-for by your family members and regular visitors, such as babysitters. Anything that needs to be accessed by all members of the household, such as frequently called numbers, takeout menus and monthly school-lunch menus, should be easily accessed from the administration station. Keep your weekly meal and chore plans here (see pages 130–131), where they can be quickly located by a family member keen to help out, and the agenda for next week's family meeting (see pages 132–133), perhaps with a pen close by so it can be added to.

An address book or plastic sleeve holding business cards or handwritten contact information can be useful, as would a password organizer with clues about passwords for accounts that are accessed by the whole family. Do not use the same password for different accounts and use a combination of upper- and lowercase letters and numbers. Use a plain address book or something inconspicuous that doesn't scream "Passwords" across the cover or binding. Prevent the wasted expense of repurchasing software, a document license or purchase information by entering serial numbers and purchase dates in the password book.

Each new school year, the same paperwork is sent home for a parent to fill in. Fill out the information once, photocopy it, then save the copies in the administration station. It's a serious sanity and time saver!

Some of the following might also be included:

- Emergency phone numbers
- Associations and organizations—contact details
- Classes—dates, times, addresses
- Sports and club calendars
- Babysitter and pet sitter information
- Home maintenance lists
- Perpetual birthday calendar
- Vacation packing lists
- Home inventory
- Gift certificates (movie theater, museum)
- Coupons (pizza, deli, takeout)

COMMUNICATION HUB
The administration station can be in any room in the house—just make sure everyone knows where it is. Keep useful pieces of information neatly packed away in a box or binder. Keep digital password reminders in a generic notebook. A chalkboard wall is a fun idea for reminders, and a place where pieces of information can be quickly noted for all to see.

Emergency phone numbers | Associations & organizations | Classes | Sports & club calendars | Babysitter and pet sitter

Overcoming procrastination

Procrastination—the act of delaying an action—is the enemy of efficiency and productivity. By decluttering our calendar, we aim to give ourselves more time, but procrastination does nothing but waste it.

We delay all sorts of things in our life for many reasons, but not all delays are procrastination. We wait to buy a house until we can afford it, or we wait and "bundle" our errands instead of making two trips. While delaying an action can be necessary or smart, procrastination is neither.

Procrastination costs us more than just wasted time. We pay the price emotionally with stress, guilt, anxiety and shame; financially, too, perhaps by incurring late fees on a conference registration or paying an extra interest to a credit-card company. Procrastination is unhealthy for our relationships because we let down the people we love and their trust in us erodes.

AVOIDANCE

Procrastinators rarely do nothing. Instead they busy themselves doing less useful things, like tidying or organizing. Both are good, but they are not to be confused with being productive. It's common for a procrastinator to get a lot done (sorting the recycling, washing the dishes) or have organized everything in their office (pens, papers, books on shelves) instead of working on a project that's due. The anticipated discomfort of starting the dreaded task preempts the anticipated "reward" feeling. Think about preparing for taxes, for example. It's easy to distract ourselves doing other things instead of gathering the required paperwork.

When this happens, it's critical to stop giving in to "feel-good" tasks. Exercise awareness and summon the willpower to get to the job at hand.

BREAK THAT HABIT
To help break the procrastination habit, organize big tasks into smaller, more manageable tasks.

4 Strategies to get you past procrastinating

One, or all, of the following strategies can help you get on with the job you are avoiding.

> ❝ When we're overwhelmed, a task is too broad, too complicated or too difficult to understand, and we simply don't know where or how to start. ❞

FEELING OVERWHELMED

People procrastinate because tasks feel either overwhelming or underwhelming. Most of the time when we're overwhelmed, a task is too broad, too complicated or too difficult to understand, and we simply don't know where or how to start. So we busy ourselves by finding something else to do instead, something that's less confusing. In this instance, rather than begin with the broad statement, "I'd like to get organized," be as specific as possible. "I want to organize my income, investments and expenses into folders for taxes."

Another reason people feel overwhelmed is because they have unrealistic expectations of themselves, others or situations. If every magazine we look at features beautifully organized, color-coordinated linen closets, it's easy to slip into thinking, "Hey, my linen closet should look like that!" We compare and judge ourselves when we don't measure up. We forget it took an entire paid staff to make the closet look that way. It's not uncommon for people to become "paralyzed by perfectionism." For some, doing nothing is better than doing a task less than picture-perfect. In this case, it is important to practice patience with yourself, and build realistic expectations. Much like the strategy of being specific and starting small, address the task in hand on a personal level, knowing what you want to achieve. For example, I don't need my linen closet to be color-coordinated, but I do need the sheets separated from the towels, or the children's bedclothes moved to the bottom shelf and my bedclothes to the top. That is achievable.

FEELING UNDERWHELMED

The opposite of being overwhelmed is to be understimulated. When a task is perceived as boring, tedious or dull, we tend to put it off. If a lack of enthusiasm is preventing you from completing a project or task, first consider the unpleasant consequences of NOT completing it. This may spur you to make a start. Bear in mind that many procrastinators overestimate the unpleasantness of a task, and by getting started you may find that it is not as bad as you thought.

1 Give yourself a deadline
Without a deadline, procrastination thrives. Anyone who has ever hosted a get-together knows how motivating it is to invite a group of people over. For several days before, there are to-dos getting crossed off lists that were ignored for months. Give yourself a reason to finish the task you are avoiding by a particular date. For example, if the guest bedroom needs decorating, make sure you have the incentive to finish by a certain date by inviting a friend to stay.

2 Give yourself a payoff
Reward yourself by doing the "worst first." For example, instead of reading the paper and drinking your morning coffee under a big, black cloud screaming, "unload the dishwasher," first empty the dishwasher and then ENJOY your morning paper and coffee.

3 2 for 1
If you know the task you are avoiding will take up your time in what seems to be both unproductive—for example, having to wait on hold on the telephone—and has no tangible goal— you've renewed your life insurance coverage but it doesn't feel like you achieved anything—come up with ways of multitasking. For example, instead of doing nothing while waiting on the phone, use the time to walk on the treadmill, do leg squats, declutter your DVR, shred junk mail or disinfect the TV's remote controls—all while listening to the recorded music on speaker phone.

4 Short bursts
Break the project down into manageable-sized pieces and work on it a little at a time. By completing quick, short tasks you will feel as if you are achieving something, and the bigger task will become less overwhelming.

MAINTENANCE

05

Once things are in place and tasks have
been identified and completed, it's time to
maintain order. This chapter sets out the habits
and routines that will help you sustain
the progress you've made.

Staying motivated

Even the most motivated of us occasionally has trouble *staying* motivated. It's hard work. The rewards are well worth the effort, but finding ways to maintain motivation means learning to overcome occasional obstacles.

Decluttering and organizing are ongoing activities, so there is always a need to stay on top of it. Fitting decluttering and organizing activities into our precious time can be especially challenging, because most days we barely manage to keep our heads above water. Below the surface we are paddling as fast as we can, coping with laundry, meals, pets, kids, aging parents, work, dishes, driving, phone calls, emails—the list goes on and on. It often feels like there's not enough time to stop whatever needs doing to start a non-priority task like sorting through outgrown clothing or inventorying the freezer.

Setting up a system of routine activities and habits (see pages 144–145), making lists of small tasks (see pages 146–147) and getting the rest of the household on board (see pages 148–149) can help with momentum, but here are a few more tips and techniques to consider when your enthusiasm is flagging.

SAVE THE GOOD BITS
Try committing to go without something: "For the next three days, I will not watch any TV; instead, I'll record the shows I like and reward myself with a show after accomplishing my goal of organizing the basement."

BE ACCOUNTABLE
If you are having trouble motivating yourself to get started, whether on a maintenance plan or a new decluttering task, try setting a public deadline, and share it with family or friends. For example, "For the next 21 days I aim to wake up an hour earlier and, before I do anything else, I will organize a category of paperwork in my filing system." Being bound by a public agreement may be the motivating factor you need.

AIM FOR GOOD ENOUGH, NOT PERFECTION
I've met many people with extreme clutter situations who have been unable to start organizing because they were paralyzed by perfectionism. For them, it wasn't worth doing if they couldn't do it perfectly.

Your friends aren't perfect, and you still like them, right? Well, you and your house aren't perfect either! Real homes don't look like the staged photographs you see on the pages of a magazine. There always will be furniture to dust, dishes to wash and laundry to fold.

Perfection is the enemy of progress. Don't let how you *think* it should be done stop you from actually *doing* it. A less-than-perfect job is much better than a task left undone. Go for good enough rather than perfect. Progress is cumulative, and organizing is a process. Every little task is another step toward your decluttering goals.

SET A TIMER
Some days you just won't feel like putting in the effort. Organizing and decluttering will seem like daunting tasks, when it's much easier to busy yourself doing something else. You're procrastinating! On days like these, a good plan is to limit the time you spend organizing. You don't have to run a decluttering marathon every day. Just a few minutes of dedicated time is better than doing nothing at all. As I have already said, progress is cumulative.

Decide how long you're going to give yourself to declutter, and set a timer, then work only for as long as the time you have set. Maybe during these short periods of time you can declutter pens and pencils from a drawer, unload the dishwasher, discard leftovers from the fridge or deadhead a plant. Focus completely on the task and avoid distractions for the time you have allocated. Give it your best shot, and accomplish as much as possible within your time limit. See page 160 for a checklist of 30 tiny tasks you can try.

HELP A FRIEND

Sometimes a little make-believe is enough to keep you motivated. If you can't find the will to declutter and organize for yourself, do it for a friend. Chances are you'd bend over backward for a good friend who has asked for help around their house. Well, treat yourself as you'd treat others, and give yourself a helping hand! Practice treating yourself as well as you'd treat your best friend.

MAKE IT A GAME

You know the cliché, "Time flies when you're having fun!" Grab a deck of playing cards. Draw a card. Go into any room of your house and do the same number of tiny tasks as the card you drew (face cards count as ten).

   You could assign each suit to a category of room, perhaps spades to bathrooms, hearts to bedrooms, diamonds to the kitchen and clubs to living spaces. For example, say you drew a three of spades: go to the bathroom and choose three small decluttering tasks to take care of.

   - Pick up loose items from the bathroom counter and put them back where they belong.
     - Wipe down the counter, sink and fixtures.
     - Empty the trash.
   Put the card back into the deck and draw another, then repeat the game in the appropriate room.

VISUALIZE

Athletes use visualization to get themselves prepared for their event. They visualize their performance and see themselves winning. Use the same technique to help you stay motivated for decluttering. Close your eyes and imagine what your home *could* look like. Visualize yourself opening your front door and walking into your home. What does the entryway look like? What does the house smell like? Is it bright and well lit? Where do you put your shoes or handbag?

Walk through your entire home in your mind. Imagine what you'd like it to look like, down to the smallest detail. You can have your dream home. It's possible. Use that imagery to stay motivated. When you find yourself tempted to give up, go back to your visualization and keep tackling tasks.

PLAY MUSIC

When I need to get motivated, I listen to music, the kind of upbeat music I can't sit still to. Create a playlist of your favorite songs, or look for one online. When you need a little extra pep in your step, press play, get up, get moving and get grooving. You can dance around the house as you declutter the tabletops and countertops. Music is motivating, and moving briskly counts as exercise.

AN OBVIOUS START

Start in the kitchen, and make your way around the house. See dishes in the sink? Place them in the dishwasher. Notice a pile of clothes on the floor? Walk them over to the hamper. Find old magazines on the coffee table? Toss them in the recycling—yes, of course you'd like to drive them to the retirement community and donate them, but you're going for good enough, not perfect, remember? When you tackle the obvious clutter first, your home will feel tidy in no time. It only takes a few minutes to motivate yourself to keep going. Once you're in motion, you'll stay in motion.

REACH OUT

At some point along the way you're going to need some encouragement. Defeatist thinking, negative self-talk or dealing with emotionally charged objects due to estrangement, divorce or death makes it difficult to process decisions or handle tasks. When doubt or isolation start creeping in, contact an accountability partner and tell them how you're feeling (isolated, overwhelmed, guilty over spending so much money on stuff you're now getting rid of, etc.). Ask for encouragement and a helping hand, whether emotional support or physical.

Creating new habits

WHERE PLASTIC BAGS GO TO DIE
Using a dedicated plastic bag dispenser may seem like a good habit to get into, but using a reusable cloth bag is a better habit.

Our habits are similar to the steps of a staircase: each personal habit either steps us up, closer to our goals or takes us down farther away from where we want to be. Sometimes we find ourselves standing still on a step, not moving up or down.

When thinking about creating and reaching goals, it's wise to review the series of small actions that need to be taken before the goal can be reached. As an example, let's agree that you've decided to stop clutter from entering your home. Break that goal into specific steps. The first small but specific step is to stop acquiring plastic bags from stores. Next, after decluttering dozens of plastic bags lurking under the kitchen sink and jammed between the fridge and cabinets, you focus on a solution to how to transport what you buy from the store to the car and into the house: you decide on reusable bags. But more important is remembering to bring the bags with you when you shop! Until that becomes a habit, it's likely that more plastic bags will accumulate and clutter your kitchen.

HABITS IN THE HOME
Developing habits can be key to maintaining your clutter-free, organized home. Just like nooks and crannies stuffed with extra plastic bags, our habits add up; they serve as reminders of our behaviors. The total of our habits become either the explanations for success or excuses for poor performance. For example, when college students make the Dean's List, it's because they've developed and practiced good study habits. When senior citizens are fit and flexible in their later years, it's not an accident; it's a result of their healthy eating and exercise habits.

One of the best ways to create a habit is to formulate multiple small but related goals. Using the plastic-bag example, instead of saying, "I'm going to declutter my house," try, "If I grocery shop this weekend, then I will use my own grocery reusable bags," which leaves more flexibility than a statement like, "I'll use reusable bags every time I shop."

When working with easily distracted, time-starved clients, I suggest they create a habit of ignoring their ringing phones. If the phone rings, let it go to voicemail. Create an "if-then" rule. "If I have a scheduled call, then I will check the phone at the appropriate time when it rings." Instruct friends, family and coworkers that if they must talk to you, they need to text/email and request phone time or schedule it in advance. For some, this advice isn't relevant (reporters, real-estate agents), but for most of us, there's rarely a reason to answer the phone. Those who want to get in touch will leave a message and then, at a time that suits you, make a list of all the calls that need to be returned and call back when it's convenient.

THE HABIT OF LISTS

One of my very favorite organizing habits is creating checklists and lists. When it comes to getting organized, whether packing for a move or a vacation, outsourcing odd jobs, or planning an event, getting into the habit of always making lists and checklists will help move you closer to your goals.

Checklists and lists serve different purposes. A checklist covers the steps needed to accomplish a goal and avoid mistakes (a checklist for working out, for example, making sure each muscle group is exercised), whereas a list can compare pros and cons (should I or shouldn't I adopt a second dog, cut my hair short, upgrade my phone) or keep track of things (all the books you've read in the past six months or the regions, sub-regions and varietals of wines you've consumed).

Creating lists and checklists helps to both reduce stress and anxiety, and to increase productivity. For example, it's easier and faster to pack a suitcase when working from a checklist. People who use lists feel more in control and prepared in emergency situations or high-risk environments. See pages 152–153 for more on making checklists to help with chores and home maintenance.

Tiny tasks

Chores are the jobs that need to be done to maintain order and hygiene in the home, but it doesn't mean we want to do them. As well as being defined as a regularly done small job, the word also describes a dull, unpleasant or difficult job, which explains how most people feel about chores.

If we wish to live in a comfortable, healthy and well-organized home (which is absolutely possible!), we have to have systems in place to make sure that all the little jobs, such as stacking the dishwasher or emptying the trash, the "monster-maintenance" jobs (perhaps painting the exterior of the house or power-washing the driveway) and all the medium-sized tasks in between, are scheduled routinely or on an as-needed basis. In the real world, however, this is more easily said than done, so my advice is to think small.

BE SPECIFIC

Most homeowners approach chores as part of their weekend routine. They create to-do lists of everything that needs to be put away, cleaned and organized on Saturday or Sunday. Many lists look something like this:
- Clean kitchen
- Organize mudroom
- Declutter living room

Look familiar? Each of those to-dos is a big job. Suddenly we realize that it's actually a big list masquerading as a little list. It feels overwhelming, and with all the other activities on the weekend (the kids' soccer games, a family reunion, a fundraiser dance-a-thon), we believe we have an overwhelming amount of work to do that simply can't be completed in one weekend.

This is when the procrastination trap opens wide and waits for us to walk right in, because it's so much easier to do other things than it is to tackle the enormous pile of decluttering projects. It's tempting to start thinking, "Maybe next weekend …"

Most to-do lists are too general and too vague. Instead, specificity works better, and big chores are best managed by breaking them up into tiny tasks.

Let's take the kitchen as an example. "Clean the kitchen" is a time-consuming task that sounds like way too much work. So, start unraveling that one to-do into multiple tiny tasks. Start in one corner of the kitchen and visually work all the way around the room. Using a notepad (or dictating into your phone), note every small step needed to clean a particular area. Here are a couple of examples:

Countertops
- Sort through the paper clutter.
- Throw away junk mail, old magazines and newspapers.
- Shred bank statements and documents containing personal information.

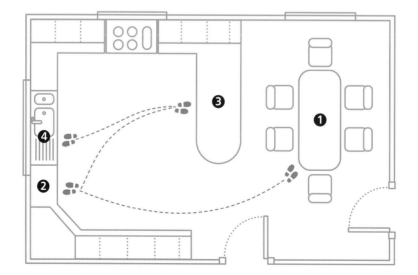

1 Clear away the dishes.
2 Fill the dishwasher, and run it immediately.
3 Wipe down and disinfect the countertops.
4 Scrub the sink, and run the disposal.

■ Take other paperwork to the appropriate area (home office, perhaps) for filing.
■ Clear away the dishes.
■ Fill the dishwasher, and run it immediately.
■ Wipe down and disinfect the countertops.
■ Scrub the sink, and run the disposal.

Already, this one big task has been divided into multiple small and achievable tasks, and you're on your way. Now let's continue.

Refrigerator

■ Clear off the front and side surfaces of the fridge, removing any takeout menus, coupons, invitations and so on. Trash out-of-date items and move the current ones (see Home Office: Action Files, page 95, and Administration Station, page 136).
■ Inside the refrigerator, check expiration dates and remove old food.
■ Pull leftovers toward the front of the shelves to be used first; this avoids wasting food.
■ Make a note of what needs to be replenished during the next trip to the grocery store.
■ Wipe down the shelves.
■ Disinfect the handles on the fridge and freezer.

Chores seem a lot less overwhelming and complicated when there's a detailed list with every task described (see Overcoming Procrastination: Short Bursts, page 139).

It's also worth keeping lists to reuse for days when "brain fog" settles in and you aren't sure what to do next. You might choose to use these lists with the timer method when you need motivation (see Staying Motivated: Set a Timer, page 142). Plus, momentum builds as you move through the to-dos. Before you know it, you'll have made progress and will have plenty of time left in the day to do what you want to do instead.

Remove any takeout menus, coupons and invitations.

Check expiration dates and remove old food.

Pull leftovers toward the front of the shelves to be used first.

Make a note of what needs to be replenished during the next trip to the grocery store.

Wipe down the shelves.

Disinfect the handles on the fridge and freezer.

MANAGEABLE CHUNKS
Break down the task of cleaning the refrigerator into bite-size pieces.

DIVISION OF LABOR
Involve the whole family, including the kids, in household tasks. Be sure to reward children who contribute.

Involving the whole family

Chore wars have been at the heart of family arguments for decades. Delegating household chores becomes even more stressful for parents who monitor progress. Let's face it, a home with kids means there's more tidying work to be done; more clutter coming home from school, birthday parties, sports games and other activities; more laundry to wash; more meals to plan; more dishes to wash; and more groceries to buy.

Even in families where both parents work, women spend almost twice the amount of time organizing as their husband. When left to only one partner, chores become a burden and can lead to family arguments. For a happier family and a healthier marriage, involve the entire family in chores and decluttering.

REWARD BOARD
Years ago, when my children were young, my husband and I decided to rename our "Chore Chart" the "Reward Board." We believe that enthusiasm is contagious. Instead of focusing on the work that needed to be done, we focused on the rewards of hard work. Our motto was "The harder you work, the luckier you get."

When children learn simple chores from a young age, they'll be able to perform those tasks on their own and accept responsibility for cleaning up their own mess. Sharing in family tasks teaches kids basic life skills, including caring for a home. Household chores will help your children feel more independent and empower them to contribute to the family in a meaningful way.

Don't forget to include adult chores on your reward board, since this helps children see that everyone is expected to contribute, and to discuss what is expected at the weekly family meeting (see pages 132–133). It is a good idea to keep the lists fairly short, so as not to overwhelm, especially for children under ten. Older kids can handle more information. See pages 164–165 for a sample chore chart and reward board.

THE RIGHT REWARD
To keep the children enthused, tailor the rewards to their interests. Pre-school children often like stickers. Try a theme: for example, they could can earn stickers of the moon and all the planets in the solar system.

When children are slightly older and in school, create a point system. After earning a predetermined number of points, each child can choose a family activity. You could watch a movie, play a board game or read a story together.

When a child turns eight or nine, you might think it appropriate to allow him or her to stay up a little later on Friday nights. If they prefer, children could earn a small reward, such as a new book.

Age-appropriate chores

As well as cleaning, tidying and organizing tasks, use the reward board to address inappropriate behavior if this has become apparent recently, or to encourage a little extra-curricular practice.

3- to 5-year-olds
- Sort laundry by color
- Place a napkin by each plate at dinner
- Use polite language
- Pick up dirty clothes from around the house
- Carry newspapers/old schoolwork/magazines to the recycling bin
- Fluff cushions on couches and chairs

5- to 8-year-olds
- Make the bed
- Feed the family pet
- Choose a healthy snack after school
- Help with folding laundry by matching socks
- Set the dinner table
- Read aloud to the dog or cat for five minutes
- Draw a picture and mail it to a relative
- Bring in firewood for the fireplace
- Fold grocery bags and put them back in the car (or wherever they are kept)

8- to 11-year-olds
- Open and close the shutters or curtains
- Clear the table after meals
- Load the dishwasher
- Put dishes away
- Wheel the trash bin to the curb
- Water flowers and help in the garden
- Unload groceries
- Do a load of laundry
- Write a thank you note or letter to a relative
- Inventory basic household supplies, school supplies or home office supplies

Hopefully, this book has shown you the benefits of a less cluttered and more organized life. You may have finished it recently or months ago. Perhaps you put it down and are rereading it to rekindle your organizing and decluttering desires because you recently started backsliding into your old, not-as-organized, ways.

However long it's been, I hope you have experienced some of the joys of being organized and less stressed. But remember that important life events can sometimes interrupt your progress. You might experience difficulty due to any number of challenges, like distractibility, sentimental attachment or procrastination. Whatever the reason, if you find yourself, little by little, slipping back into old habits, allow yourself to be your own best friend. You know, the one who is compassionate and optimistic; the one who talks you in off the ledge when you experience disappointment and want to emotionally beat yourself up.

POSSIBLE CAUSES

The tip of the clutter iceberg might start with an innocent Saturday-morning shopping trip. You stop at a yard sale (or two) and pick up a few items. Next weekend you hit a flea market and buy a few things that will go into your dream home—someday. Later that week, you purchase maternity clothes online that you don't need for a few months. That weekend, your neighbor brings over her old maternity clothes for you to borrow but your online order has already been shipped. You're working extra hours and don't make time to return the maternity clothes, so they ride around in your car for a couple of weeks. Paperwork for your first-grade twins comes home in their backpacks. It's already time to register them for camp, and if you do so within 21 days,

you save 10 percent. But before you can return the forms, you need to call the pediatrician and have the doctor sign a form stating they're up to date on vaccines. Meanwhile, it's too late to return the extra maternity clothes you bought online. Every night you are tired after dinner, dishes and baths, so anything extra that requires attention instead sits on the counter. And there's laundry, grocery shopping, lunches, gymnastics, birthday parties—and you're tired, really tired.

For some people, backsliding starts small. It might be hormonal shifts, an unresolved conflict, a new and exciting relationship, social pressure or any number of things that allow us to justify a drastic behavior. For others, something big triggers a behavior binge, for example, spending more time than we planned playing computer games, watching TV or perusing favorite social-media sites.

YOU CAN GET BACK ON TRACK

One of the most important things to do is to recognize backsliding when it occurs. Realize that it's not unusual when there's a break in your new routine—such as the holidays, a vacation or hosting houseguests—for old

How to cope if you

habits to resurface. Acknowledge what's happening, rather than ignoring, denying or rationalizing it. Try to reboot and recommit to both decluttering and organizing. Make an effort to remove as many temptations or triggers as possible, because the longer you're exposed to them, the greater the probability of backsliding.

Finally, step back and realize that a relapse is nothing more than a wrong turn. You are in control and simply need to recalculate. Get back on the road and keep heading in the right direction.

backslide

REVISIT AND REASSESS

The key to handling backsliding is to be aware of what's going on so you can diagnose and prescribe by revisiting the advice given in this book.

Are you procrastinating? Review Overcoming Procrastination (see pages 138–139) to establish what you are avoiding and why, and adjust your mindset to get you through it. You could also try a few motivational techniques or games from Staying Motivated (see pages 142–143). Are your closets and drawers full? Revisit the pages on bedrooms, closets and linen closets to find specific advice relevant to your situation (see pages 74–87 and 106–109) . Too busy for any of this? Refer to the Calendar Clutter chapter (see pages 124–139) and take a day to unschedule events you, regretfully, have committed to.

Last but not least, credit yourself for deciding to read this book and exploring the many ways decluttering and organizing will enrich your life and make your home warm and welcoming.

SEEKING ASSISTANCE

If you are truly feeling lost and are experiencing prolonged periods of feeling overwhelmed, ask for help. You can call on the services of professional organizers to deal with the clutter in your home, while therapists can help you deal with the clutter in your head.

Professional organizers have a wide variety of specialties, with areas of expertise ranging from home organizing to productivity boosting. Most organizers will answer questions over the phone to determine whether they can be of help to you. They'll inquire about your particular organizing challenges. If they can't help you, they'll refer you to an organizing colleague or a therapist.

Use these questions when interviewing professional organizers to make sure you find someone who matches your needs, and is an accredited professional.

■ What are your areas of expertise? Possible answers may include: clients with ADHD; time management; wardrobes and closets; financial matters; computer-related challenges; speaking; coaching; writing; estates; seniors; home staging; or relocation.
■ Are you certified? By whom?
■ Are you insured?
■ Do you attend conferences or tele-classes and stay abreast of current trends and techniques?
■ Do you have local references? (Talk to previous clients.)
■ Do you belong to any professional organizations? (A professional affiliation demonstrates a commitment to the field and is another way to check up on reputation.)
■ How long have you been in business?
■ What hours do you work? What days of the week are you available? (Make sure that this person's availability is a good match for your availability.)
■ Do you bring the necessary supplies, or do I purchase them separately?
■ If you purchase supplies or materials at a discount, do you charge an "up charge" or an hourly shopping fee?
■ Do you make arrangements to take away any donations, consignments and trash? If so, do you charge a fee for this service?
■ Do you work alone, or do you have a team of employees or subcontractors?
■ Do you have advertising on your car? (Ask this if you want discretion; some do not want coworkers or neighbors to know they've hired a professional organizer.)
■ Do you take photographs on my property? (If privacy is a concern, tell the organizer you do not want your home photographed.)
■ What is your fee, and how do you charge? (Options may include hourly, by-the-project or bulk rates.) What is your policy on a retainer, cancellation fees and minimum number of hours?

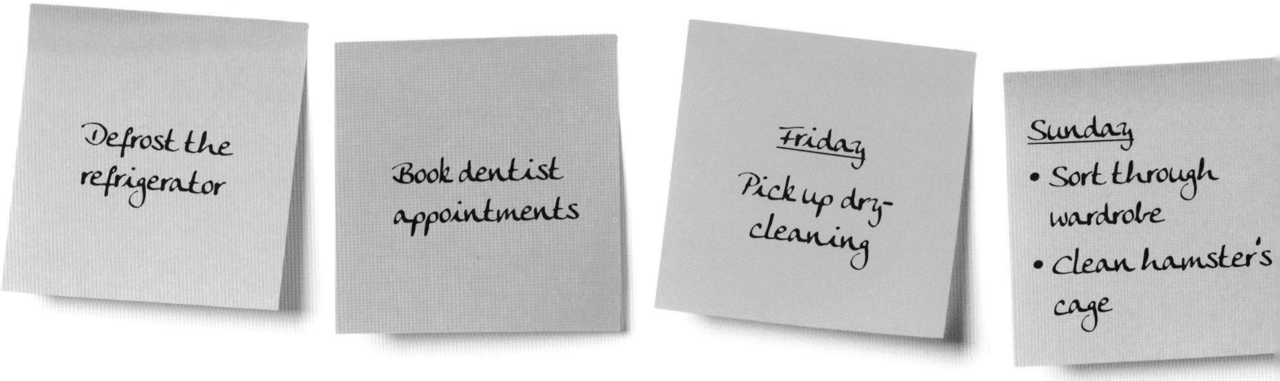

Defrost the refrigerator

Book dentist appointments

Friday
Pick up dry-cleaning

Sunday
- *Sort through wardrobe*
- *Clean hamster's cage*

Making checklists

As we have already discussed, routine chores are a necessary part of maintaining a well-ordered home, and doing a few each day prevents the need for a marathon decluttering session over the weekend. By implementing a variety of checklists for household chores that need to be done daily, weekly or seasonally, you'll spend your Saturdays and Sundays playing and resting instead of scouring, spraying, scrubbing and scraping.

I've broken my chore lists into three intervals: tasks that need to be completed every day, every week, and when the seasons change. You can use my actual list (see pages 158–159) or create your own list based on your home situation.

Daily chores are those that require the minimum amount of work to keep your home humming and hygienic, such as washing dishes, picking up clothes, wiping down surfaces and making the bed.

Weekly tasks ensure your home is clean and organized for the next week: disinfecting, changing sheets and pillowcases, doing the laundry and vacuuming. If doing all your weekly tasks on one day is too much, divide them up throughout the week (see also Tiny Tasks, pages 146–147).

Seasonal chores are done infrequently and therefore require a little more time. Sometimes they require calling in professionals, such as having the dryer vents or chimney cleaned. I like to reserve four weekends each year for the do-it-yourself seasonal tasks.

LIST IT TO GET IT DONE

One of the benefits of having detailed checklists is that nothing is forgotten—ever. Checklists help us stay on track, and tasks that must be accomplished are more likely to get done regardless of everything else going on in our lives. Plus, they help things become more routine, which is an important process in habit formation. Checklists are critical to keeping homes clean, decluttered and organized all the time—not just in the cleanup scramble before guests arrive.

The Checklists and Planners chapter (see pages 154–169) is a great resource of checklists and templates you can use to keep your home and home life decluttered and organized.

Spring tasks
- Mow lawn
- ~~Paint fence~~
- Weed garden

Saturday
Change and wash
master bedding

Amelia's turn to do
the vacuuming
this week

Thursday
Clean bathroom

4 Make your lists work for you

Here are some ideas to make using your checklists easier and more efficient.

1 Schedule time

Life can become hectic unexpectedly. If you find yourself putting in extra hours at work or attending to more family obligations, chores are among the first things to go. It may help in the short term, but putting household chores on the back burner is a mistake. Believe me, a clean home will make you a happier, more productive person—and it only takes a few minutes each day.

To see this tip through, keep your priorities focused by blocking out time on your calendar (see Prioritizing, pages 126–127, and Saying "No," pages 128–129). Don't assume you'll fit it in between dinner and bedtime. Make time. Let your family know so they won't interrupt you. Better yet, give them tasks, and have everyone pitch in (see Involving the Whole Family, pages 148–149).

2 Keep cleaning supplies close

There are two approaches to this. You can store your cleaning supplies in a bin and carry it from room to room, or you can keep cleaning products in various locations around the house—utility rooms, laundry rooms and under sinks usually work best. If the supplies you need are close at hand, you can quickly wipe over the sink or clean the mirror, and tick a chore off your list in seconds. If dragging your vacuum around the house is too laborious, consider keeping a handheld vacuum with your supplies for on-the-spot cleanups.

3 Post your lists somewhere visible

Laminate a printed chore list, and hang it in a closet or on the inside of your medicine cabinet. It will serve as a daily reminder to keep you accountable. Store a dry-erase marker close by to check off items as you complete them.

4 Good enough and you're done

Chore lists are meant for quick cleanups. Don't worry about being too thorough. Instead, limit each task to 10–15 minutes. Remember, perfection is the enemy of progress. This is especially true for daily and weekly tasks. If you miss something, you'll get it next time.